MEN'S ACTIVISM TO END VIOLENCE AGAINST WOMEN

Voices from Spain, Sweden and the UK

Nicole Westmarland
Anna-Lena Almqvist
Linn Egeberg Holmgren
Sandy Ruxton
Stephen Robert Burrell
Custodio Delgado Valbuena

First published in Great Britain in 2021 by

Policy Press, an imprint of
Bristol University Press
University of Bristol
1–9 Old Park Hill
Bristol
BS2 8BB
UK
t: +44 (0)117 954 5940
e: bup-info@bristol.ac.uk

Details of international sales and distribution partners are available at
policy.bristoluniversitypress.co.uk

British Library Cataloguing in Publication Data
A catalogue record for this book is available from the British Library

ISBN 978-1-4473-5618-9 hardcover
ISBN 978-1-4473-5619-6 paperback
ISBN 978-1-4473-5621-9 ePub
ISBN 978-1-4473-5797-1 OA PDF

Cover design: Robin Hawes
Front cover image: Stocksy
Bristol University Press and Policy Press use environmentally responsible
print partners.
Printed in Great Britain by CMP, Poole

For this and future generations of activists

Contents

List of figures

Notes on authors

Anna-Lena Almqvist is an Associate Professor in Social Work at Mälardalen University, Sweden. Her research interests focus on work–family balance, families with two mothers and youth in complex life situations, often in a comparative perspective. She has published her work on young people in *Community, Work & Family* (Taylor and Francis, 2018) and on the role of partners and workplaces in relation to parental leave decisions in *Men and Masculinities* (Sage, 2017).

Stephen Robert Burrell is an Assistant Professor (Research) in the Centre for Research into Violence and Abuse (CRiVA) in the Department of Sociology, Durham University, UK. Stephen has carried out research on the prevention of men's violence against women, masculine gender norms, masculinities and COVID-19, and undertaken an ESRC Postdoctoral Fellowship on the business sector's role in violence prevention.

Custodio Delgado Valbuena is a Professor of Sociology in the Department of Sociology, Seville University, Spain. He is interested in the sociology of gender, education and social inequalities and men and masculinities. He has published a number of books, chapters and articles on these subjects. He was co-founder of the first Men's Group of Seville, a member of Red de Hombres por la Igualdad in Spain and a member of MenEngage Europe.

Linn Egeberg Holmgren is a Senior Lecturer in Social Work at the Centre for Social Work, Department of Sociology, Uppsala University, Sweden. Her research interests consist of interactionist theory, interview methodologies and men's profeminist work. She has worked as an expert advisor in surveying gender equality interventions focusing on men, boys and masculinity. Her PhD research was on men as feminists, and she has also published on researching men and masculinities.

Sandy Ruxton is an independent consultant and Honorary Research Fellow in the Department of Sociology, Durham University, UK. He has conducted men and masculinities research for a range of organisations including the European Institute for Gender Equality, the European Women's Lobby, Oxfam, the Open University, the British Council and the Government Equalities Office. He is a member of the Steering Committee of MenEngage Europe.

Nicole Westmarland is a Professor of Criminology and Director of the Centre for Research into Violence and Abuse (CRiVA) in the Department of Sociology at Durham University, UK. Her previous books include *Violence against Women* (Routledge, 2015), *Researching Gender, Violence and Abuse* (Routledge, 2018), *International Approaches to Rape* (Policy Press, 2011) and *International Approaches to Prostitution* (Policy Press, 2006).

Acknowledgements

We are grateful to all who have supported us in the preparation of this book, including the research advisory group, research participants, our work colleagues, university administration staff and our personal family and friends. The research was made possible through funding from the British Academy (Grant number SG151643).

1

The need for men's involvement

Men's violence against women and girls is a problem crossing all social groups. Globally, it constitutes a leading cause of the premature death of women and children, with its impacts ricocheting far into all communities (Westmarland, 2015). Many have argued that men must engage further in the movement to end violence against women. However, there is relatively little knowledge available about structural and individual factors that might enable and support this engagement. This book aims to develop an understanding of the factors that enable men to actively take a stance against men's violence against women. Based on a survey and in-depth interviews with men who are involved in this work in three European countries (Spain, Sweden and the UK), we explored the men's own personal backgrounds and motivations as well as asking them to act as 'experts' in understanding which factors (personal, socio-cultural, political and/or economic) might encourage and support more men to become active.

This is a field of research that we as authors have been involved in in a variety of ways for different lengths of time. The research project leading up to this book initially came about through discussions between Nicole Westmarland, Sandy Ruxton and Keith Pringle, with others joining the project as it progressed. The research was funded by the British Academy. We had two core research questions that we set out to answer:

1. What are the personal backgrounds and life experiences that lead some men to actively and publicly challenge men's violence in society?
2. What are the socio-political, personal, political and economic factors that are conducive to enabling and supporting more men to do so?

This chapter outlines why this topic is important and describes the research methods we used to investigate it, as well as the rationale for our focus on Spain, Sweden and the UK. It then provides a brief background of the men who took part in the research. Finally, it provides an overview of key international research, and considers the unique contexts of the three different countries focused upon.

Why research men who take action against men's violence against women?

It has become increasingly recognised in recent decades, both within feminist movements and in wider society, that it is important for men to speak out about men's violence against women (Flood, 2019). Flood (2011) argues that there is a powerful feminist rationale for involving men in such efforts: they are predominantly responsible for the problem in the first place, in terms of its perpetration; violence against women is built upon social constructions of masculinity and on men's structural dominance across the different levels of society; and men also have the potential, currently largely untapped, to play an important positive role in helping to end violence against women. Indeed, given the first two points, they could be seen as having an ethical responsibility to do so (Pease, 2002).

In Spain, Sweden and the UK, along with many other countries, the 1970s was a key decade in which the Women's Liberation Movement raised awareness about the pervasiveness of such violence and started to establish women's refuges, shelters and rape crisis centres in a quest to keep women safe. Since then, the feminist movement has diversified, expanded and been highly influential in a range of academic, policy and practice advances. What to do with the men who perpetrate such violence and abuse has been a much slower conversation, and this has stilted attempts to reduce or end men's violence against women. We concur with Hearn in *The Violences of Men* (1998) where he highlights that, when it comes to violence against women, it is men who are the 'specialists' in its use. As a group of researchers working and writing together, we strongly believe that the way to speed up the ending of men's violence against women is to substantially scale up our efforts, bringing on board far greater numbers not only of women and girls but, crucially, men and boys. Understanding more about the pathways men currently involved took and their views on the opportunities and challenges to increasing these pathways is an important step in achieving this.

Our project

We used existing men's organisations and networks to recruit participants for either an online survey or an in-depth interview. In total, we had 40 respondents to our survey, while 24 men participated in interviews. We specifically approached men and organisations that we wanted to recruit into our study rather than using snowball or other more open sampling techniques. The individuals and organisations were approached because we saw them as being particularly influential and important representations of men's anti-violence efforts in the three countries. Although recruitment would have substantially increased if we had used social media networks, there was concern within the research team about how the sample might become skewed in certain directions if we opened up recruitment in this way. This was particularly the case for the survey, given its anonymous nature. For the in-depth interviews, the reason for not using wider sampling methods was due to needing to limit the sample for resource reasons (we only had funding of £10,000 for the study across all three locations). In addition, we intentionally wanted to keep this as an in-depth study of those men who participated in the interviews.

We attempted to recruit a diverse range of different men, especially for our interview sample, but we are aware that the data will not be representative of all men involved in work of this nature across the three countries. Instead, this book aims to start a discussion – to act as a springboard – on the issue of men's activism in ending violence against women in Europe.

We adopted a broad approach to defining men's activism. During the research, we stated that we were looking to speak to men who take a public stance against men's violence towards women, for example by organising or participating in events, giving talks, speaking out through social media, raising awareness within organisations and multi-agency fora, organising campaigns, going on marches, undertaking or delivering training on these issues, being a spokesperson in the media or holding political leaders to account. It is important to note that this could also involve 'everyday activism' in one's personal life (Sowards and Renegar, 2006), for example by speaking out and challenging sexism, misogyny and violence towards women among friends, family and peers. Activism also does not have to mean explicitly political activities; it could involve taking action through one's professional work, for example, such as being highly committed to tackling men's violence against women as a police officer or social worker.

It is also important to note that there is more than one approach from men towards gender politics, and some of these can be harmful, anti-feminist and misogynistic. Flood (2007) argues that the loosely defined 'men's movement' can be understood in terms of five overlapping strands of agendas and understandings:

- Men's liberation (focuses on the damage, isolation and suffering experienced by boys and men through being socialised into manhood).
- Anti-sexist or profeminist (acknowledges men's pain, but gives greater emphasis to male privilege and gender inequalities).
- Spiritual and mythopoetic (influenced by Jungian psychology, especially the work of Robert Bly, and sees masculinity as based on deep unconscious patterns and archetypes revealed through myths, stories and rituals, which should be explored so men can restore their psychospiritual health).
- Christian/religious (bringing men together through Christianity or other religious beliefs to embrace more 'Godly' influences in their world − often evangelic, fundamentalist and favouring a return to traditional gender relations, for example, the Christian Promise Keepers).
- Men's rights and fathers' rights (blaming women and feminism for harms done to men, denying ideas about male power and privilege and arguing that men are now the real victims of social injustice).

This research focuses primarily on the second strand (which Flood contends is the smallest in many contexts), as it is within anti-sexist and profeminist politics that men's activism to end violence against women typically (though not always) falls. Flood notes that such groups frequently distance themselves from the broader 'men's movement', which they often perceive to be defending male privilege.

All of the authors of this book (plus Keith Pringle from the original research team) conducted interviews for the study, some by men and some by women. Our sample is not large enough, and we are too diverse a group of researchers (in terms of nationality and level of experience/seniority), to be able to comment on what impact the sex of the interviewer had on our data collection (interviews particularly) or analysis. However, it would be naive to think that these and other differences had no impact. As Egeberg Holmgren (2011a, 2013) notes in her study on profeminist men in Sweden, there are many complex interactions in terms of power that exist within qualitative interviewing. This is particularly the case in studies such as this one where the interviewer and interviewee have overlapping or similar positions − 'a common language and knowledge at hand in the interview situation'− which she names a 'discursive closeness' (Egeberg Holmgren, 2011a: 366–7). Once the interviews had been carried out, transcripts were thematically analysed (Braun and Clarke, 2006) by teams in each of the three countries before being brought together to assess similarities and differences across Spain, Sweden and the UK.

We are grateful to a research advisory group made up of representatives of non-governmental organisations (NGOs) and academics who supported us throughout the fieldwork stage of the research. Ethical approval for the study was granted by the Department of Sociology (then called the School of Applied Social Sciences) Research Ethics Committee at Durham University.

Why choose Spain, Sweden and the UK?

Choosing which countries to focus on in a study is often mediated by more than one factor. In-depth, PhD research had fairly recently been carried out in the UK and Sweden, by Wright in the UK (and then also by Burrell) and by Egeberg Holmgren in Sweden. We knew there were groups of men that were active in both of these countries – in Sweden we had links with MÄN and in the UK with organisations such as the Good Lad Initiative and the White Ribbon Campaign. Attendance at a conference in Barcelona by Westmarland opened up Spain as a third site of interest after she witnessed a group of men holding a candlelit memorial in a central location in Barcelona for women killed through men's violence. Connections were also available with NGOs across all three countries through the European section of the MenEngage Alliance. Hence, the three countries were chosen in part due to similarities (we knew they all had non-profit organisations who were active in the area of men's involvement in ending violence against women and we knew they all had academics studying this field, including ourselves), in part due to practicalities and resources (the original investigators on the grant were located in two of the three countries) and in part due to differences (we knew that approaches to gender equality work and violence against women differed across the countries, as well as important political, social and economic factors such as the timing and the impact of the preceding global recession).

Another important difference is that each country broadly reflects one of Esping-Andersen's (1990) three main types of welfare regimes, with Spain close to a conservative/corporatist welfare state (shaped strongly by traditional family values), Sweden representing a social democratic welfare state (based around universalist services promoting an equality of high standards) and the UK reflecting a liberal welfare state (featuring limited, means-tested support for those with the lowest incomes). This has significant implications for gender relations, the provision of services and broader social and political discourses in each country. For instance, in Spain, caring responsibilities are more likely to be delegated to the family, and in particular, the mother. In Sweden, the universalist approach to welfare means that the state plays a greater role in care. In the UK, the market is more influential, affecting the quality of care provided outside of the family and who has access to it.

There have been subsequent updates to Esping-Andersen's typology, with research suggesting that Mediterranean European countries such as Spain form a fourth 'southern' regime type based around a more rudimentary, fragmented welfare state which is heavily reliant on the family and voluntary sector, and with less commodified societies (Bambra, 2007). Feminist theorists have also argued that an accurate analysis of welfare regimes should take gender into account much more prominently than Esping-Andersen did. Instead, his focus was primarily on the labour market in terms of decommodification (the extent to which people can survive without participating in the labour market) and levels of social stratification.

For example, Trifiletti (1999) utilised Esping-Andersen's concept of decommodification, but added an analysis of gender discrimination (based around the extent to which the state considers women to be wives and mothers or workers) to make the case for this 'Mediterranean' welfare regime type. Trifiletti argues that Mediterranean welfare regimes such as Spain have a high level of gender discrimination, but unlike conservative or 'breadwinner' welfare regimes, also provide little support for families. Despite the criticisms of Esping-Andersen, the social policies of Spain, Sweden and the UK typically fall into distinct categories within other typologies of welfare states, including when gender is explicitly taken into account (Bambra, 2007). As researchers, we were keen to observe whether these kinds of gendered systemic issues and policy differences between the three countries had any impact on the experiences and pathways of the men that we interviewed.

Backgrounds of interview participants

The 24 interviews were conducted with a range of different men involved in ending violence against women in Spain, Sweden and the UK. Most were in middle age, with the age groups of 45–54 and 55–64 most represented, although some were younger (including a few in the 25–34 category), especially in the Swedish sample. Most of the interviewees were well educated, with almost all having a Bachelor's degree and some having Master's degrees or PhDs; in some but not all cases, these were in gender studies or a related subject. Several of the men were doing paid work related to anti-violence efforts, including within NGO contexts, as freelance trainers or consultants, as university lecturers/professors or in government institutions. This was not the case with all interviewees, however, others had occupations including writers, retired or students. The majority of interviewees lived in large urban environments, though some of the British men in particular lived in small cities or towns.

Generally, the interviewees were originally from the countries that they were based in, although some of the Swedish men described possessing multiple national identities. This was also more complex among the Spanish participants, with some describing themselves as Catalan, or being both Catalan and Spanish or Basque and Spanish. Similarly, in the UK we interviewed participants from Northern Ireland and Scotland as well as England.

Several of the Swedish interviewees described themselves as having multiple ethnic identities or heritages. This was less frequent in the British and Spanish interviewees, who were predominantly (though not exclusively) from a white ethnic background. This may reflect a lack of diversity in men's anti-violence work in these countries, though, more broadly, Spain is also a less diverse country than the UK and Sweden. Most of the interviewees described themselves as atheists or having no religious affiliation, although a few were agnostic, one British man was Muslim, one Spanish man was Buddhist and another Catholic.

While most of the participants did not report having a disability, three did: one Swedish man described himself as having autism and ADHD (Attention Deficit Hyperactivity Disorder), one of the Spanish interviewees had chronic fatigue and another was permanently unable to work. The interviewees had a range of sexual orientations; most identified as heterosexual, but a minority did identify as being gay, bisexual, pansexual or queer, and one identified as being non-binary.

Backgrounds of survey respondents

40 men who identified themselves as taking a public stance against violence towards women completed the survey. 18 of these lived in Spain (45 per cent), 11 lived in Sweden (28 per cent) and 11 lived in the UK (28 per cent).

Most survey respondents were middle-aged or older, with the largest number (12–30 per cent) being 55–64 years old. 11 of the respondents were aged 35–44 (28 per cent) and nine were 45–54 (23 per cent). Fewer respondents of a younger age took part, with six being 25–34 years old (15 per cent) and none being younger than 25. Meanwhile, two were aged over 65 (5 per cent). As with the interviews, the majority were highly educated, with ten having a Bachelor's degree (25 per cent) and 25 being educated above this level (63 per cent). Four were educated to the level of college or sixth form (10 per cent), and one to the level of secondary school (up to the age of 16).

The survey respondents identified as taking a public stance about men's violence against women did so in a range of different roles, and in multiple ways at the same time. 23 were doing so as part of paid work (58 per cent), 21 as an activist (53 per cent) and 12 as a volunteer (30 per cent). Some of the respondents provided more specifics about their role, with one mentioning that he was a police officer, and another explaining that he was 'using [his] position as a Professor to study and spread the message against men's violence against women, and the need of boys and men in engaging in gender equality issues'. Some responses highlighted that the reality of men's roles in speaking out about men's violence against women can sometimes be more complex. One commented that he had 'started out as an activist but ended up within paid work', while another remarked 'the way I live my life!'. This also raises the question of what counts as activism, given that everyday acts in one's personal life can be just as important as organised and public political practices. For instance, one respondent wrote that for decades he was 'extremely committed' to the men's profeminist movement but is 'nowadays taking a break' and 'using social networking sites but not taking part in men's groups. I'm just aware of issues', while another simply commented 'as a father of 3 sons'.

The fact many respondents selected more than one option for this question demonstrates that the boundaries between paid work, voluntary work and activism in this field can often be blurred, or put into practice at the same time. Indeed, this is something which the authors can relate to as well; being a feminist or profeminist academic also often involves doing paid work, voluntary work and activism simultaneously – and it's not always clear when one begins and another ends.

Previous international research

Looking internationally at this field, we see men involved in a range of networks and organisations to increase gender equality and reduce violence against women and girls across the globe. Some of the most well-known include Promundo (originating in Brazil), Sonke Gender Justice (South Africa), the White Ribbon Campaign (originating in Canada), HeForShe (led by the United Nations) and the global MenEngage Alliance. However, many countries now have their own organisations or networks dedicated to this type of work (Hearn, 2015).

Research into the men involved in such networks and organisations is more limited, however, as it is for women's involvement in feminist and anti-violence work. One possible reason for this is that, given the enormity of the task at hand (ending men's violence against women), such projects could be seen as less important at best or as 'navel gazing' at worst. Most of the studies to date, however, do have a focus not only on documenting the 'stories' of those involved but also on how this knowledge can be used to encourage or support others to join the movement. In our research, the in-depth interviews were equally divided in terms of time and questions related to (1) backgrounds, motivations and obstacles faced by the men in terms of their own stories and (2) what needs to be done in terms of changing social structures to encourage more men to become involved.

In 2009, Egeberg Holmgren and Hearn highlighted the need for more empirical studies into men's different profeminist positions in order to strengthen and develop theoretical work on this topic. Of studies published in the English language, the largest empirical research projects on this topic have mainly been conducted in the US. However, there are also smaller in-depth studies that have been undertaken elsewhere, including the PhD research of two of the authors of this book (Egeberg Holmgren in Sweden and Burrell in the UK). Theoretical engagement with the topic, along with attempts to raise its status on the political agenda, have also been strong in other parts of the world, especially in Australia (Bob Pease, Michael Flood, Raewyn Connell, to name a few).

One of the most significant studies about men who are 'allies' to the feminist movement to end violence against women is that by Messner, Greenberg and Peretz (2015) in the US. They carried out 64 life history interviews with 52 men as well as 12 women aged between 20 and 70 involved in anti-violence activism in North America. Their research suggests that there are three different generational 'cohorts' of men who have engaged with feminism and work to prevent violence against women at different historical moments. The men in these cohorts share some commonalities in their pathways into this work as a result. The three groups they describe are: the 'movement' cohort, who became involved in anti-violence work from the mid-1970s to the mid-1980s; the 'bridge' cohort, from the mid-1980s to the mid-1990s; and the 'professional' cohort, from the mid-1990s to the present day. These shifts in the nature of men's involvement are closely connected with changes that have taken place in the wider feminist movement. Messner, Greenberg and Peretz (2015) emphasise the importance of men's 'moments of engagement' in shaping these pathways – when and through which cohort they came into contact with feminism and violence prevention work, rather than how old they are.

For men in the 'movement' cohort, there were four key experiences that shaped their pathways: being part of a generation who were immersed in social movement activism (such as the anti-war and New Left movements); having close connections with feminist women; being involved in men's consciousness-raising groups and then in profeminist networks; and responding to challenges from women and from feminism. For men in the 'bridge' cohort, they appeared to have more varied pathways, and represented an increasing diversity of backgrounds (with many men in the earlier 'movement' cohort being white and middle class, by contrast). In addition, these men were influenced by feminists becoming increasingly involved in organisation-building, becoming more professionalised and working more within institutions such as universities, but potentially with less of a politicised focus on social change. Within this cohort, there also began to be more of an attempt to reach out directly to men, while still retaining a critical feminist lens in relation to men's position within patriarchy.

Finally, in the 'professional' cohort, men have been becoming involved at a time in the US which has seen a growing network of non-profit organisations working on violence prevention (including engagement with men and boys) and further professionalisation of this work, as well as some degree of marketisation, as organisations compete for government and foundation funding. This has meant that more men are doing anti-violence work on a paid basis and, the authors argue, some have even become individual entrepreneurs gaining some degree of 'rock star' status in the field as a result. This professionalisation appears to have further expanded the diversity of the bridge cohort, as well as the number and range of men's pathways into violence prevention work. For instance, for men who had prior experiences of racism and poverty, this shaped how they came to be involved in and how they practice profeminist work, and meant that they brought with them a more 'organic' intersectional analysis connected to their own experiences of oppression.

Messner, Greenberg and Peretz (2015) argue that there may be an emerging 'social justice' paradigm within this work, building on the public health paradigm of the 'professional' cohort. This has three core features: the influence of feminist professional networks within anti-violence work providing an important source of activism and critique; the rise of 'organic intersectionality' based around some men's own experiences of different forms of oppression, as cohorts have become more diverse; and the emergence of transnational networks of individuals and organisations working in violence prevention. However, it is important to highlight that most countries have not seen the level of professionalised, funded work to prevent men's violence against women that the US has; for Spain, Sweden and the UK, the processes that Messner, Greenberg and Peretz describe may have been happening more slowly and on a smaller scale.

Another key US study is that by Casey and Smith (2010) who interviewed 27 men who had recently become involved in an organisation or event dedicated to ending sexual or domestic violence. They found that initial 'sensitising' exposures to the issue of violence and the experiences of survivors, combined with how they understood these experiences and tangible opportunities to become involved, were key. For these men, the pathway towards anti-violence activism was a process which unfolded over time, and which featured a number of different influences – it was never shaped by a single factor, but through a combination of experiences and reflections. It was typically based upon the issue of violence against women becoming personally relevant to their own lives in some way, or through making an empathetic connection of some kind with the emotional impacts of abuse.

Casey and Smith (2010) discuss the importance of existing personal connections and social networks for the men they spoke to in facilitating their initiation into violence prevention work. Important links were also made by the men between their activism and a sense of community, either in terms of perceived support from existing communities that they were a part of, or as a way to build a new sense of community for themselves.

In another study based on a survey of men who had attended events focusing on the prevention of violence against women, Casey et al (2017) found that the most frequently reported explanations for becoming involved were: concern for related social justice issues; exposure through their work to the issue of violence; hearing an emotionally impacting story about abuse; or listening to a disclosure of abuse from someone in their lives. Casey et al (2017) developed four profiles to classify men's motivations for initiating their participation in violence prevention. These were based around having different connections to violence and abuse:

- Low personal connection, for example becoming involved through other social justice issues or through their employment.
- Empathetic connection, for instance by hearing disclosures of abuse from people in their lives, or learning about violence against women through presentations or on the internet.

- Violence exposed connection, through personally experiencing, witnessing or using violence.
- High personal and empathetic connection, by having personal experiences of violence and seeking out learning opportunities and the stories of others.

Interestingly, there did not appear to be significant differences in how long someone remained involved for the men who fell into each of these different categories (Casey et al, 2017). This suggests that these different profiles of motivation may each be similarly impactful in getting and keeping men involved in anti-violence work.

Also in the US, Peretz (2017) has cautioned that it is vital to adopt an intersectional approach to the question of why men become involved in efforts to prevent violence against women, otherwise there is a risk of making inaccurate universalisations about men's experiences. His research on men's pathways into campaigning for gender equality demonstrates that these may be less homogenous than the existing literature suggests, especially for men who themselves experience forms of oppression and marginalisation. For example, Peretz found that within a gay and queer men's gender justice group, their pathways typically began earlier than most. They were not as reliant on the influence of women in their lives and did not create a shift in their gendered worldviews. This was because their own intersecting identities and experiences meant that they already had more of a connection to gender justice than most men. As a result, these men often lacked a traditional 'pathway' narrative. Peretz therefore points out that men's pathways into profeminist and anti-violence activism are shaped not only by their identities as men, but also by their other intersecting identities and positions. These may blend experiences of privilege on one hand with marginalisation on the other, or multiply different forms of privilege in their lives.

One significant piece of international research is the IMAGES (International Men and Gender Equality Survey), which is one of the most comprehensive efforts to gather data on men's attitudes and practices related to gender equality. This focuses on eight low- and middle-income countries: Brazil, Chile, Mexico, India, Bosnia and Herzegovina, Croatia, Democratic Republic of Congo and Rwanda (Levtov et al, 2014). The survey provides a picture of men's attitudes towards gender and gender equality, explores what the determinants of more equitable attitudes might be and investigates the associations between equitable attitudes and behaviours in relationships. A total of 10,490 men aged between 18 and 59 completed the survey between

2009 and 2012. One of its findings was that higher levels of education and income, and experiencing more equitable practices at home when growing up, appear to be associated with men having more equitable attitudes and behaviours (Levtov et al, 2014). Furthermore, in most countries, men who had more equitable attitudes were also more likely to engage in more equitable practices, such as greater participation in childcare and domestic duties and lower levels of intimate partner violence perpetration. They also reported having higher levels of satisfaction in their sexual relationship with their partner, suggesting that equitable attitudes among men do not just have positive effects for women, but also for men themselves (Levtov et al, 2014).

A later IMAGES study by Heilman, Barker and Harrison (2017) in the US, UK and Mexico with nationally representative studies of young men aged 18–30 went on to explore certain conceptions of masculinity and the extent to which these influence young men's ideas of what is means to 'be a man'. The majority of the men interviewed supported the idea of gender equality and affirmed that men should be encouraged to engage in what were once considered to be traditional female activities, such as childcare. However, many also equated being a man with using violence to resolve conflicts, refusing to seek help even if they needed it and sticking to rigid gender roles. A smaller qualitative study in the UK by Robb and Ruxton (2018), which contributed to the overall IMAGES study and was based on a series of focus groups drawn from a diverse cross-section of the community, also found that many young men accepted gender equality in principle, although in some cases their attitudes and behaviour lagged some way behind their expressed beliefs. Many still experienced pressures to conform to rigid and stereotypical notions of what it means to be a man, but they increasingly expressed scepticism towards and detachment from those stereotypes. Moreover, this research provided evidence that gender roles and relationships can change and develop, suggesting the possibility of more positive and fulfilling gender identities for the next generation of boys and young men.

Flood (2019) builds on Casey and Smith's (2010) findings and argues that there are four main factors which are particularly important in influencing men's initial entries into anti-violence work: personal 'sensitising' experiences which raise their awareness of violence against women and/or gender inequality; invitations for involvement; making sense of their experiences in ways which have a motivational impact; and their social conditions. Sensitising experiences can make the issue of men's violence against women more real or pressing in some way, such as by learning from women (often a family member or friend) about violence and abuse that they have suffered – or indeed having direct experiences of violence themselves. It could also involve having connections with or mentoring from particular women, as well as the influence of peers, both of which can help to cultivate a deeper understanding of injustices experienced by women and the need for men to take action. As highlighted by Peretz (2017), involvement in the cause could be influenced by men's own intersectional identities, which may involve their own experiences of oppression and inequality. In addition, Flood (2019) contends that some men's pathways into anti-violence work are influenced by pre-existing commitments to social justice and rejections of belief systems that justify social inequalities. In this respect, exposure to or education in feminist and anti-violence ideas and understandings can also play an important role.

The second key factor Flood describes is that of having opportunities for involvement in anti-violence work, be that through activism, a job or a local group (Flood, 2019). Formal invitations into such activities, for example from friends or other members of the community, can play an important role here. Third, Flood highlights the importance of meaning-making: the meanings men give to initial experiences of sensitising events and involvements in anti-violence activities. The research by Casey and Smith (2010) found three main themes in these meanings: being compelled to action (no longer feeling able to do nothing, and believing that they can make a difference); having a changing worldview (involving shifts in their own thinking in relation to violence against women and how it connects to their own lives and to wider society); and anti-violence work being a way to join with others (in terms of finding a way to build community and mutual support with people who share similar beliefs, and who 'do' masculinity in alternative ways). That said, for men who themselves already have experiences of oppression, encounters with feminist ideas may be less characterised by shifts in meaning, and more with acquiring an enhanced language to express existing understandings.

Finally, Flood (2019) emphasises the importance of wider social conditions in shaping men's opportunities for becoming involved in work to end violence against women. This can include the contemporary social context of feminist and women's movements, violence prevention work and government policy in a specific setting. As a result, the nature of men's pathways and involvement in anti-violence work can change according to this wider social context.

We next go on to look at research that is specific to the three geographical locations that this book covers – Spain, Sweden and the four countries that make up the United Kingdom (England, Scotland, Wales and Northern Ireland).

The Spanish context

A key historical moment in Spain was the transition from Franco's totalitarian regime in 1978 to a more democratic and decentralised political system, and the subsequent re-building of civil rights and democratic institutions, which the women's liberation movement played a significant role in. The Catholic Church has traditionally played a major part in influencing the configuration of laws in areas such as education and shaping political and moral debates in Spain, however after the fall of Franco, the women's movement was able to campaign successfully for civil rights such as divorce (in 1981) and abortion (1985). Since then, the participation of women in the labour market has increased rapidly, and a strong feminist movement has been built (Bustelo, 2016; Lombardo, 2017). Three key moments in this regard were the first National Days for the Liberation of Women in Madrid in 1975 (the same year Franco died), the Granada State Feminist Conference in 1979 and the creation of the Spanish Institute for Women in 1982. The latter has subsequently played a central role in bringing gender equality issues into mainstream politics and into Spain's legal and bureaucratic structures, which some have described as a form of 'institutional' or 'state feminism'. The first shelters for victim–survivors of domestic abuse were also established in Spain in the 1980s, in Madrid and Pamplona in 1984 and in other communities from 1986.

Following the 1978 constitution, Spain has become a quasi-federal state made up of 17 Autonomous Communities, with enormous regional diversity and significant nationalist movements, making gender policies highly decentralised and largely dependent on the Autonomous Communities (Alonso, 2015; Bustelo, 2016). Recently, the Great Recession starting in 2007 had a particularly significant impact, especially for Spanish women, who are more likely to use and work in the austerity-hit public sector or in caring or informal sectors. However, between 2004 and 2011, several progressive laws against gender-based violence and increasing civil rights were implemented while the PSOE (Spanish Socialist Workers' Party) were in power. Since 2016, the feminist movement has been galvanised, particularly as a result of a high-profile gang rape (the 'Pamplona gang rape', discussed in Chapter 4) and the mobilisation of protests after the trial for that case. There has been, for example, a feminist strike in 2018 supported by 5.5 million people, with rallies involving 3.3 million (mainly women but also some men), and massive feminist demonstrations every year on International Women's Day since 2017. These have led to some improvements in legislation, around sexual assault laws for example.

However, there has also been backlash against these movements, including from the rise of the far-right in Spain, primarily through the Vox Party, which has espoused anti-feminist and misogynistic discourses and values. In the 2019 general election, Vox gained the third largest number of votes. They have campaigned against pro-gender equality budgets and a specific law to tackle violence against women, and have put pressure on Partido Popular, the main conservative party in Spain, to go backwards on gender equality issues. This is one example of how, in countries across Europe, political polarisation has increased in recent years, including in relation to gender equality policies.

Men's groups have existed in Spain since the 1980s as a space to encourage men to question their own sense of masculinity and male privilege, create new ways of enacting or constructing masculinities and become involved in taking action for gender justice and against violence towards women (Lozoya et al, 2003; Delgado Valbuena, 2006). Bonino (2008) has argued that Spain has the largest amount of profeminist men's groups and activities in Europe; in 2008, he wrote that there were at least 19 groups across the country, and this figure has subsequently grown substantially. Bonino and other authors have therefore contended that Spanish profeminist men's groups are a somewhat unique phenomenon, with greater numbers and impact than many other countries. Alongside this, during the first two decades of the twenty-first century, there has been an increase in studies on men and masculinities which have been mainly written in Spanish and not translated into English, building on the pioneering early work of figures such as Josep Vicent Marqués (1991). These include theoretical and personal accounts such as: Lorente Acosta (2008, 2009, 2018), Bonino (2008), Lozoya, Bedoya and Espada (2008), Delgado Valbuena (2009), Guasch (2012), Salazar Benítez (2013), Coronado (2017), Azpiazu (2017), Bacete (2017) and Téllez Infantes (2019). Others are empirical studies such as the series of surveys developed by the Ministry of Equality's Delegation of the Government Against Gender Violence (Ministerio de Igualdad, 2020). These are important to note because of the considerable impact they have had on Spanish speaking communities around the world, particularly in Latin America.

Over time, men involved in smaller collectives became members of broader groups which started to develop at the end of the 1990s and into the 2000s following a series of conferences held in different Spanish regions (in Seville and Jerez in Andalusia, Donosti in the

Basque Country and Barcelona in Catalonia). The two main umbrella platforms of profeminist groups are Red Hombres por la Igualdad (RHXI) [Men's Network for Equality] and Asociación de Hombres por la Igualdad (AHIGE) [Men's Gender Equality Association] which joins with other individuals such as those working in perpetrator intervention programmes, politicians and academics to make up the Movimiento de Hombres por la Igualdad [Men's Movement for Equality]. As is common in social movements such as these, the actions and priorities of individual men and groups varied and were largely independent of government funding, at least in the early days. For example, the first March of Men against Violence against Women was held in Seville in 2006 and in 2011 Barcelona hosted the Ibero-American Congress on Masculinities and Equality (CIME), which included most of the men's groups in Spain and some representatives from Latin America. This involved the development of the 'Barcelona Manifesto'; a commitment from the conference delegates to an agenda for change for gender equality, including the denunciation of all forms of male violence and establishing more egalitarian and caring masculinities. These conferences and marches have played an important role in enabling a range of people (including men's groups, activists and academics) to come together, and can provide a key 'moment of engagement' with anti-violence work for some men (Delgado Valbuena, 2006), as some of our interviewees pointed out.

There have been a few books published in Spain which document the 'stories' of men taking action against violence towards women and for gender equality. For instance, Guash's (2012) edited collection uses the life histories methodology to explore the lives of 12 men who in various ways challenge models of manhood centring upon toughness and being a breadwinner. Meanwhile, Coronado's (2017) edited collection catalogues the stories of men working in different areas of Spanish social life to end violence against women, based upon 16 in-depth interviews.

More recently, using ethnographic methods, Nardini (2016) looked at the ways in which men network for gender justice in Italy and Spain. Like Delgado Valbuena, she describes a wide range of non-profit organisations being active, with AHIGE having local delegations in most Spanish cities, and the Men for Equality Forum organising activities in Seville, for example. Nardini also describes Government-led initiatives which exist both on a local and regional level, such as the Gizonduz project created by Emakunde, the Basque Women's Institute. This has developed a range of initiatives to engage more men in building gender equality, including through the prevention of violence against women and promoting fathers' involvement in caregiving. The first government-funded programme to work with men was developed by the Municipality of Jerez de la Frontera in Andalucia in 2001. This was developed after a conference in the same city, and was led by one of the members of the group Men of Sevilla; it is still working today, and served as a model for later programmes, such as Gizonduz and another developed by the Municipality of Barcelona.

Although many of the groups within the Men's Movement for Equality have a wider remit than gender-based violence, Nardini reports that involving men in speaking out against violence towards women is often one of the main objectives and closely linked to their wider gender justice aims. As an example, she explains that among AHIGE members violence is referred to as 'violencia machista' which links the violence to 'cultura machista' – a culture which has machismo at the heart of norms around what it means to be a man.

In her study of the men involved in some of these groups (as well as those in Italy that she also investigated), Nardini concludes that men have no linear path into profeminist activism and advocacy, that they usually start with developing anti-patriarchal beliefs and then begin a personalised journey. She found a commonality across the men in her study of the importance of seeing men and boys as potential change agents and understanding themselves as being gendered, writing: 'Acknowledging the social construction of normative masculinity among men is pivotal for making visible its relation to men's practices that lead to violence' (Nardini, 2016: 254).

In 2018, a process of internationalisation began, whereby Spanish members of the MenEngage Alliance saw the potential for developing their social networks and gaining knowledge, diversity and experience from other European counties. This led to the launch of MenEngage Iberia in June 2019 in partnership with Portuguese organisations working with men and boys. This includes a range of different organisations, including the aforementioned RHXI, AHIGE and others such as Fundación Cepaim, as well as Promundo Portugal and the Portuguese Associação Para o Planeamento da Família [APF – Family Planning Association]. This, combined with the development of the MenEngage Europe network more broadly, has provided important opportunities for connections, exchange and learning with other organisations across Europe (including some in Sweden and the UK).

The Swedish context

In Sweden, the feminist movement has been able to establish a strong gender equality discourse in Swedish politics in recent decades (Nyberg,

2012; Martinsson et al, 2016). This has led to significant policy developments such as the introduction of paid parental leave (from 1974) leading to a month being reserved for fathers in 1995; a growing movement for women's shelters during the 1980s (which are today run by state-funded NGOs); and the prohibition of prostitution and the pioneering of the 'Nordic model' (which criminalises sex-buyers and decriminalises women in prostitution) in 1999. All of these can be considered part of what is described as Swedish 'state feminism', which is to some extent characteristic of social democratic welfare state regimes, with the women's movement operating more 'inside' the state than is perhaps the case in Spain or the UK (Kantola, 2006).

Political debates, as well as the Nordic research field since the 1980s and 1990s, have also had a strong focus on including men and boys in efforts to build gender equality, as evidenced by the emphasis on issues such as fatherhood and parental leave arrangements (Lundqvist, 2013). For example, Sweden has some of the strongest and most gender equal parental leave policies in Europe. The total number of days of leave parents can take from the workplace is 480 per child, and of these 90 days are non-transferable 'daddy days' to encourage men to use parental leave. National as well as regional information campaigns during the 1990s and early 2000s encouraged fathers to use parental leave in an effort to increase shared responsibility for children. To speed up fathers' use, a third month was introduced in 2016 (Kaufman and Almqvist, 2017). Sweden was the first country in the world with a shareable parental leave in 1974 and yet, there are still further steps to go; while men are taking more leave days than ever (more than 30 per cent according to the Swedish Social Insurance Agency, 2019), women still do the majority of childcare and often work part-time during the child's pre-school years. Furthermore, research indicates that fathers are more inclined to take part in and share childcare compared with carrying out household chores (Almqvist and Duvander, 2014).

The extent to which the discourse about including men and boys in efforts to build gender equality is anchored in actual practice is therefore questionable at times (Pringle, Balkmar and Iovanni, 2010; Pringle, 2016). However, the impact of gender equality and anti-sexist discourses in Sweden (including in the political sphere, for example), together with the influence of feminist activism, may have paved the way for younger men to engage positively with these ideas to some degree. Some participants in this study will have thus grown up in a context where it is almost taken for granted that boys and men will espouse gender equal and anti-sexist values.

However, these discourses have historically left issues of men's violence largely unaddressed. Compared to Spain and the UK, the emphasis of the women's movement and government policy in Sweden has traditionally been oriented towards gender equality more broadly rather than violence and abuse (Pringle, 2005). It has also been argued that the policy focus on fathers' parental leave has led to other gender equality issues being marginalised (Järvklo, 2008). Yet this has been changing in recent years, where awareness has grown and there has been more of an emphasis on taking action to stop men's violence towards women, including at the policy level (Statens Offentliga Utredningar 2014, 2015). The #MeToo movement against sexual violence appears to have had a significant impact on Swedish society, for example.

The primary organisation in Sweden working with men and boys to build gender equality, MÄN (which translates simply as 'men'), dedicates a significant portion of its efforts towards ending men's violence against women. MÄN was established in 1993, originally with the name Män för Jämställdhet – Men for Gender Equality. They undertake a range of different forms of work with men and boys across Sweden around the themes of violence prevention, promoting equal parenthood, changing masculine norms, providing support to young men and organising local community activities. They also play a leading role internationally, such as in the MenEngage Alliance and its European network. MÄN contributed to a Swedish government report on men and gender equality which mapped out non-governmental organisations working with men and boys (Män för Jämställdhet, 2014), and concluded that most organisations are small, non-profit and focusing on violence prevention.

Most studies of men engaging in feminism, gender equality work and violence prevention in Sweden have been performed at undergraduate level (cf. Kjellberg, 2013; Kamyab and Geborek Lundberg, 2019) and in smaller postdoctoral projects (Ekelund, 2020). One of the few more extensive studies about men engaging in feminism, some of them working to prevent violence against women, has been conducted by Egeberg Holmgren (2011a, 2011b). She carried out qualitative interviews with 28 young men aged 20–34 in Sweden who identified as 'feminist', exploring their gendered and gender political positions and practices. Egeberg Holmgren discusses the complex and ambivalent issues involved when men attempt to 'do' feminism, as they enact their gendered position in different social settings – especially contexts of feminism and in social relationships between men, where the combination of masculinity and feminism can become contradictory. She highlights unique features of the Swedish context, in which there is a qualified social consensus on gender equality, and a broadly positive place accorded to men's relations with feminism (Egeberg Holmgren and Hearn, 2009). In this environment, support for men's participation in the Swedish gender equality project (in particular as white heterosexual fathers), contributes towards the construction of men as potentially 'new' and 'good' gender equal feminist subjects.

Egeberg Holmgren (2007; Egeberg Holmgren and Hearn, 2009) describes ways in which profeminist men enact 'passing', a micro-sociological process in which their positions as men and feminists in their everyday lives are made authentic, at the same time as they attempt to manage their masculinity, particularly in homosocial environments. In analysing their presentations of self, Egeberg Holmgren discusses how the ambiguous meanings of men's profeminist positions emerge, illustrating the multi-faceted ways in which men might simultaneously do, undo and redo feminism. This incoherence of the subject can be managed through 'passing' strategies which can be devised to manage what is causing men's sense of deviance, be it masculinity or feminism. This means that men may simultaneously become more feminist in practice, and as a way to 'pass' in certain contexts. Such strategies can highlight processes of distancing from other men, but also expressions of self-reflexive suspicion and sometimes seeing oneself as complicit to patriarchal structures.

Egeberg Holmgren (2007) describes how radical feminism and radical constructionism intersect in these men's attempts to make their feminist positions comprehensible to themselves and to others. However, within the context of gender equality, this may also leave men in a contradictory position, out of place in a kind of 'no man's land', where they feel unable to attain the expectations associated with either masculinity or with feminism. Egeberg Holmgren's research highlights that as with other men, profeminists have made considerable investments in masculinity as a social resource, which can lead to contradictory positions and the politics of 'passing' to cope with contexts where these two things appear incompatible (Egeberg Holmgren and Hearn, 2009).

The UK context

In the UK, the emergence of the second wave feminist movement in the 1970s and 80s resulted in small numbers of 'anti-sexist' men engaging with this new terrain. This involved men setting up consciousness-raising groups to explore sexual politics and their relations to patriarchy, and some actions in support of women's rights (eg in relation to abortion and childcare). These efforts were documented and discussed in the ground-breaking journal *Achilles Heel*, which was launched to coincide with the London Men's Conference in 1978 and ran until 1999 (see Seidler, 1991). Women often had mixed feelings about these developments, questioning whether they amounted to a reassertion of men's power in the face of feminism (Delap, 2018). But these nascent initiatives helped to highlight issues which over time became more prominent on the public agenda, such as fatherhood, gay rights and men's violence.

From the 1970s onwards, the increasing focus within radical feminism on men's violence, both against women and children, contributed to this becoming a major area of policy, practice and research concern. It has been suggested that this is the field where UK initiatives have made the greatest contribution to research on men and masculinities within Europe (Pringle et al, 2006). Until the twenty-first century, most of the work in this area centred around either domestic violence perpetrator programmes (coordinated by the national umbrella body Respect which was launched in 2000) or around the White Ribbon Campaign, part of the international movement that encourages all men to wear a white ribbon and make the promise to never commit, excuse or remain silent about male violence against women (Ruxton and van der Gaag, 2013). However, since the mid-2010s, some other groups have started to become active in encouraging men and boys to reflect on and create change related to tackling gender inequality, violence against women and dominant ideas of masculinity. Perhaps the most well-known example of this is the Good Lad Initiative (now called Beyond Equality), which runs workshops in universities, schools and workplaces to engage men and boys in building gender equality. There are also more localised groups such as A Call to Men UK, Future Men and initiatives around the Mentors in Violence Prevention programme first developed by Jackson Katz in the United States (Burrell, 2018).

The women's movement has made significant strides in getting men's violence against women onto the agenda and improving policy and practice in the UK in recent decades (Hester, 2005). This has included building one of the strongest networks of feminist, autonomous rape crisis centres and domestic violence refuges (the first of which opened in Chiswick, West London in 1971) in the world (Harne and Radford, 2008; Westmarland, 2015). These have subsequently developed into professionalised specialist services with some degree of public funding. However, they have been weakened in recent years as a result of neoliberal government austerity measures in the wake of the 2008 Great Recession; the influence of marketised, 'gender-neutral' approaches to tackling violence and abuse through depoliticised, generic services; and the continued under-prioritisation of men's violence against women as a social and public health problem, with the emphasis placed solely on criminal justice responses (Ishkanian, 2014). This has inevitably had a knock-on effect on violence prevention work with men and boys too, with such efforts remaining fragmented and small-scale in the UK, even if they have also become better connected internationally in recent years through the MenEngage Alliance (Burrell, 2018). It is also important to remember that the UK is not one country but four, and that there are significant differences in the gender equality politics and policies of England, Scotland, Wales and Northern Ireland. For example, Scotland has typically adopted a more progressive approach to promoting gender equality and tackling men's violence against women (Lombard and Whiting, 2015). Meanwhile, gender relations in Northern Ireland continue to be influenced by the fallout from the 'Troubles', the ethno-nationalist, sectarian conflict which took place between 1968 and 1998.

One of the first studies on men taking part in profeminist activism was that by Christian (1994), who carried out 72 life history interviews with 30 men who were supportive of feminism and involved in anti-sexist men's groups in the UK. This was with the aim of understanding more about how anti-sexist men are 'made'. Most of the men Christian interviewed had early life experiences with unconventional features, departing in some way from traditional gender expectations. This included non-identification with traditional fathers; identification with nurturing fathers; experience of strong mothers, who were usually involved in paid work; parents who did not conform to conventional gender roles in the home; the influence of older sisters or brothers; or childhood friendships with girls, or friendships in situations where gender was de-emphasised. In addition, many of Christian's interviewees had had an adult experience of feminist influence, typically in the form of a close relationship or friendship with at least one woman who was actively feminist.

Christian (1994) argued that his research showed that feminist ideas have had a significant impact on at least some men, and that individual feminists can have an important personal and political influence in relationships with individual men. However, he also noted that it is unlikely that all men will respond to such an influence in the same way, and that pre-existing fertile ground is likely to be necessary for feminist influence to occur, in terms of early life experiences which prepare boys to relate to women in more equal ways. Almost all of Christian's participants were heterosexual men, so he contended that it is important to avoid over-generalising about this group, because his research demonstrated that it is not only feminists and gay-liberation activists who are opposed to hegemonic masculinity. He therefore argued that non-macho, non-gay identities which exist among men and boys need to be better highlighted and distinguished; something which this book seeks to contribute towards.

More recently, Wright (2009) carried out an institutional ethnography about the work of men within the domestic violence sector in the UK. This included 17 interviews with men involved in the field, as well as attendance at thirty public and semi-public events across the country around the theme of men's violence against women. Most of the men Wright spoke to also reported having women in their lives – for example family members or partners – who had actively encouraged an awareness of gender inequality in them. She argues that this can be conceived as a form of everyday activism within a framework of resistance on the part of these women, building more equal gender relations on an individual basis. Meanwhile, Wright notes that while all of the men who participated in her research were proactively committed to their work, there were also four main problematic elements of their practice.

First, Wright contends that the potential for recognition and prominence is significantly higher for men than it is for women within the domestic violence field. She found that the small numbers of men from which male representatives can be drawn in the sector has opened up a space which facilitates the occupying of key positions by men, and this can enable personal gain, the production of knowledge seen as 'expert', and involvement in vital decision-making. This does not mean that men will necessarily 'take over' or exploit these positions, yet Wright did note many instances where men's voices were valued over women's voices in such contexts. Second, while most of the men were focusing on changing men's practices, many of them were only comfortable with doing this to a certain extent, and expressed hostility towards forms of feminism that they deemed to be too 'radical' or 'extreme'. For example, in their group-work programmes, some of the men risked feeding into opposition towards feminism among participants by masking, hiding or subsuming feminist ideas.

Third, Wright found that several of the men were in the process of developing men-only groups with questionable political commitments and practices. Some of these groups, which gravitated towards 'mythopoetic' movements for example, emphasised countering the costs of patriarchy for men, and rebuilding homosocial relationships, while lacking a corresponding political recognition of the privileged position of men in the gender order. Finally, Wright described how some of the men's practices could be interpreted as resembling 'gender tourism' or 'forced entry', in which feminist theory was in some ways appropriated by the men, and used for their own gains without moving beyond exploitative gendered relationships in their own lives. Wright observed this in some of the rationales for the men-only groups, for example, being based upon the feminist conception of women's consciousness raising, despite the origins of these groups being rooted in the idea of women sharing their experiences of male oppression.

Burrell (2019) has also conducted research into efforts to engage men and boys in the prevention of men's violence against women in the UK. This included interviews with 14 people who have played an influential role in developing this work, of which 13 were men. For many of these interviewees, the presence of feminist women in their lives had a significant impact on them and played a central role in shaping their world views. Burrell questions the notion that men and boys will only listen to other men when it comes to taking on board profeminist and anti-violence messages, or that it should be men's voices which are prioritised when it comes to engaging with other men and boys. He points out that women are already playing a key role in both formal and informal efforts to encourage men and boys to take on board feminist ideas and think critically about gender and violence (even if it may sometimes be more in 'behind the scenes', less public-facing roles which receive less recognition), and that this should not be underplayed.

Furthermore, Burrell notes that the influence of feminist women in men's lives clearly has an impact on their attitudes and practices, given that many of the men he interviewed cited this as being the primary factor in why they got involved in efforts to end violence against women. Ruxton et al (2019) make similar arguments in their research on young men in the UK and the influence that male role models have in their lives, challenging the assumption that role models for young men and boys have to be men, or that it is male role models who inevitably have the most decisive influence as they grow up. They argue that it is unclear what the meaning and function of 'male role models' might be, and how the process of modelling operates in practice, despite the elevation of the idea of 'male role models' as being all-important in wider society.

Burrell's (2019) study also highlights that it is important not to essentialise the reasons for men's involvement in efforts to end violence against women, as if some men have always held such beliefs, that they are born with them or that some men are 'inherently' more progressive or profeminist in some way. This can create false dichotomies between men and blur the complex and contradictory nature of men's practices within patriarchy, as if some are clearly, inevitably and always 'good' and some are inevitably 'bad'. Instead, one key factor may be the extent to which men and boys are able to have opportunities to question norms of masculinity in their lives, explore alternative ways of being a man as they grow up and face fewer pressures to conform to certain gender expectations. He suggests that if boys and young men are not discouraged from behaving in emotionally sensitive, empathetic and caring ways as they grow up, for example, they may in turn be more open and supportive towards ideas of gender equality later on. In addition, many of the men Burrell interviewed had an existing involvement in political activism and a commitment to social justice, which played a key part in leading them towards taking up profeminist and anti-violence ideas.

This book

The rest of this book covers three main topics. Chapter 2 looks at the ways in which men become involved in activism and work to end violence against women. For most, although not all, of the men this was a process, and these journeys are described for the men in our research and compared with what is known from previous research. Following that, Chapter 3 looks at the experiences of men once they are involved in men's activism to end violence against women. The socio-cultural and political contexts of Spain, Sweden and the UK are significant here, and the data are considered in relation to these backdrops. Chapter 4 focuses on the opportunities and the barriers to getting more men involved. Finally, we bring together the main themes that have run throughout the book in Chapter 5, and consider what more needs to be done.

2

Becoming involved

Why and how some men become active in speaking out about men's violence against women is a question which arouses considerable interest and curiosity. Yet it is a topic there has been relatively little research on to date, even though critical studies on men and masculinities has grown considerably as a field of research since the turn of the century. Where research has been carried out in this area, it has largely been based on contexts such as the United States and Australia rather than on European countries. Most of the data within this chapter comes from the interview sample, although we draw on the survey data where relevant.

In line with previous research outlined in Chapter 1, in nearly all cases (though with some notable exceptions where men were catapulted into the work following a family tragedy), men's involvement was a process rather than a particular epiphany, and the men were able to trace their involvement through a number of influences in their child and adult lives.

First, we will discuss our survey findings on why it is so important that men take a public stance against violence against women.

Why should men take action?

There are a number of potential benefits to men taking action against men's violence towards women – for women and girls, for wider society and for men and boys themselves (Jewkes, Flood and Lang, 2015). We asked our survey respondents about what they felt the main positive outcomes were. The options which had the highest levels of agreement (ie from all or almost all respondents) were: 'safer, freer lives for girls and women' (75 per cent strongly agreed, 25 per cent agreed), 'contributing to the building of gender equality' (73 per cent strongly agreed, 28 per cent agreed) and 'an important step towards ending violence against women' (75 per cent strongly agreed, 23 per cent agreed).

There were high levels of agreement with the other options too: 'sexual relationships based on consent' (53 per cent strongly agreed,

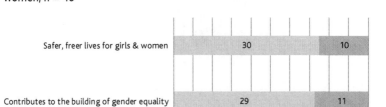

Figure 1: Possible benefits of more men taking a public stance on violence against women, n = 40

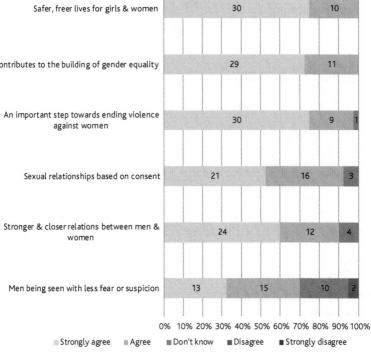

50 per cent agreed) and 'stronger and closer relations between men and women' (60 per cent strongly agreed, 30 per cent agreed). There was more uncertainty about 'men being seen with less fear or suspicion' – 25 per cent were unsure about this and 5 per cent disagreed (although the majority still agreed that it was a benefit). This may be because some respondents were uncertain if this would be a consequence of men speaking out, or were not confident that this should be seen as important compared to the positive impacts for women and girls.

The respondents suggested a range of other advantages to men taking a public stance against violence towards women, too. One UK respondent wrote that 'It would encourage more men to speak out who agree, but who are worried about how they will be seen by other men if they speak out.' A Spanish respondent added that 'Men should take a stance to fight heterosexist violence, therefore homophobic violence should be part of the same claim, and violence against feminist men and those who don't agree/fulfil hegemonic male chauvinist roles and values.' One respondent made a powerful point about the impact it can have on other men around them:

> I think other benefits include: providing a positive role model to other men in relation to violence and abuse or gender equality. Or, at least, problematising aspects of men's identity while at the same time taking a public stance on violence against women – for example, I have a lead local authority role with responsibility for partnership work around domestic and sexual violence and violence against women and girls. I am also an out gay man. I think that means I can demonstrate alternative ways of 'doing' masculinity which may help other men to question their beliefs, attitudes etc. (UK)

Several respondents focused on the positive impacts for victim-survivors, with one commenting that it 'makes children safer in their home. Not exposed to domestic violence' (Sweden), another stating 'creating an atmosphere in which women who come forward with experiences of VAWG [violence against women and girls] are more likely to be believed and supported' (UK) and one arguing that 'it provides support and reassurance to victims that there are men who are against VAWG' (UK). Some respondents also highlighted the message it sends to wider society, such as how it 'increases societal messages more generally about unacceptability of domestic abuse' (UK).

Others pointed to wider societal impacts too, including 'equalising the justice gap between genders. Making women feel less like second citizens' (UK). Another wrote that 'there is a general benefit of a social nature that is derived from the policy towards care and collaboration and the distance from competitiveness. A free society needs equality and fraternity to be complete' (Spain), while one felt that 'if we take a public stance we will erode years of 'men being in charge'. This will move us to have a more equal society' (UK). Meanwhile, one Spanish respondent stated that it can have 'benefits for peace, solidarity and social development'.

Finally, some respondents illustrated that there can also be important benefits to men themselves when they take a public stance against violence towards women, such as 'improving men's life quality' (Spain). One felt that it can lead to 'greater self-confidence, security and freedom in the men themselves' (Spain) while another pointed out that it 'makes men more free from stereotypes' (Spain). Similarly, one respondent wrote:

I think that there are benefits to men in terms of them being able to live free from the stereotypes of what it is to be 'male' which, in turn, should help them to live more fulfilling personal and professional lives which should have a positive impact on their mental and physical wellbeing. (UK)

However, a Spanish respondent provided an important reminder that none of these potential benefits are inevitable as soon as men start speaking out about men's violence against women:

Men assuming collective responsibility/accountability for violence against women. All the above only if men who take a public stance really walk the walk and not only talk the talk, and if other men follow their example. (Spain)

Next, we will discuss the key factors among the men we interviewed that influenced them to become involved in activism to end violence against women.

Mothers, grandmothers, partners and other women in the family and community

For some of the men we interviewed, the relationship they had with their mothers was, in different ways, an important one in terms of understanding their involvement in anti-violence work. This could be either a positive or a negative driver towards involvement. For the participants for whom it was a positive driver, this was most often linked to having a mother who brought their children up within an explicitly or implicitly feminist household. Dean, from our UK cohort, was a good example of this:

My mother was always very committed to various forms of fairness and equality. In her behaviour, the way she treated myself and my brother and sister, she was very even-handed in everything she did. She wasn't passing on or enforcing strong gender stereotypes. She herself was very frustrated by the world she had grown up in which assumed she'd be a stay-at-home mother. She wasn't happy about it and complained to me about it during my childhood. I felt comfortable with those discussions and understood what she was going on about. (Dean, UK)

For some men however, it was seeing how their mother was treated negatively – either by their father or by other men that prompted their involvement. Sometimes this was linked to parents separating and/or being brought up by a single mother and the injustices they witnessed and associated with this. Mothers, and in some cases grandmothers, were seen as being 'inspirational' in these men's childhoods for various reasons such as taking challenging pathways through life (either by choice or not). For example, Jack, one of the Swedish participants, talked about his grandmothers being an inspiration, one of them having a challenging life as house-wife and the other going back to education late in life to become a priest. At that time there was great resistance to women becoming priests in the Swedish protestant church and therefore she experienced great prejudice and difficulties in doing so. Another described being raised by his mother after his father (still unknown to him) left when he was a baby. He remembered his mum having friends he described as 'quite tough who had been through a lot' (Robert, UK), overhearing discussions about feminism, men's sexism and the presence of renowned feminist magazine 'Spare Rib' around the house.

Some men were inspired by the way their mothers fought to find their own ways and spaces, for instance after a separation. Although the experience might not always have been an easy one, the eventual impact on themselves was one they came to value greatly. In this quote, Noah recalls how he perceived his mother changing when his parents separated from the perspective of himself as a disapproving teen:

> So well, I got to stay with my mother. And then she had sort of postponed putting herself in the first position in life, basically all the time of her life. And then she had like an epiphany, that 'Well, I'm going to study' […] And she went to [university town] during the week, and basically… I lived with my bags packed, moving around at different friends for the better part of my year as a 14-year-old, which is basically the year everything happens that shouldn't happen. And it happened when both my parents were gone. To me, it was like … I never even thought of it as my dad letting me down, because I just took for granted that he wasn't around. But my mother, who had been around, she is the one who emotionally I put the blame on. And it was also, 'Okay, she's doing this to work with women, rather [than staying with me]'. So, I had some time where I would sit in my bedroom at home as a child, where I would feel resentment to the idea of the women's movement, the

feminist movement. And then, basically, I just dealt with that when I was 20-something. (Noah, Sweden)

Noah goes on to further reflect on how experiencing his mother's development during his childhood years later made him re-evaluate and take another, more positive stance towards the women's movement when dealing with his feelings and experiences in his twenties:

> I was aggravated by [mother going into studies] because she really developed, if you like. It's a preposterous thing to say as a kid, but when you see that one of your parents is really blooming and also, I guess you could say, maturing. And then I just felt that 'No, that's not something that I should put blame on', or 'that's not something that has jeopardized, threatened me, it's just been something that has been beneficial'. So, it went from, what do you call it? Truce, to becoming peace, to becoming a kind of welcoming of and a curiosity about it. So, I grew from being sceptical … not hostile, but sceptical, to becoming rather enthusiastic and positive (Noah, Sweden)

The influence Noah is describing is based on the experiences he has understood in retrospect rather than at the time, re-evaluating how blame was directed towards the mother but not the father. He goes on to explain how his mother 'bloomed', finding truce, peace and eventually curiosity about the choices made by his mother and the feminist movement.

Sometimes it was not only the mother or grandmother, but also other women in and around the family being seen as particularly strong.

> There were some very, very strong, women within my family circle, and I think that's always, helpful. Individuals who set the culture and expectations around the family. And so there were lots of men around as well, but it wasn't just about a male agenda, or a male culture, there was certainly always a very strong culture which was about a women's place, which meant I was also prepared to challenge others who saw women's place as being narrow, rather than, broader. (Christopher, UK)

As well as the 'strong women' within his immediate family circle, Christopher grew up in Northern Ireland during the 'Troubles', and witnessed women as mothers, grandmothers, sisters and as wives coming together to try and put pressure on paramilitary groups to stop them using violence. He recalled that this was particularly influential. Some groups, such as Peace People, encouraged women to come onto the streets – in the first instance about paramilitarism. However, in bringing women together, such groups also provided a focal point to talk about other issues that they were facing. This 'power of women coming together' was part of the process for Christopher of developing the profeminist, anti-violence stance that he went on to take into his practice as a social worker and youth worker (which were also linked to an important personal experience and an influential university lecturer, described in later sections).

Female partners were also described as powerful influences on the men's pathways on a number of occasions, even if the intimate relationship later ended. Swedish interviewee Patrik reflected on the importance of men having and being impacted by close relationships with women:

> Well, I think that one common denominator for men who have been engaged in this question like for real, I think at least most of them they tell a story about a woman who has challenged them. Often it's in a close relationship and has something to do with love, that you care about what that person says and you understand this is important. So, I think that it's something that is crucial. But at the same time, how do we get men to go into close relationships? Not to just be heteronormative now, but most are in a relationship in some form or other. The question is how do you get them to at least open a small door, to feel something and be close? Because I think that is a key factor. (Patrik, Sweden)

For two of the men from the Swedish cohort who placed the greatest emphasis on relationships with intimate partners in their journey towards anti-violence activism, both later lost those relationships with much heartache. Yet this did not detract from the immense impact these relationships had on their long-term process towards challenging men's violence to women.

Several of the men also talked at length about the influence of feminist women with whom they had very close platonic relationships. Again, this was usually pushing their development forward in significant ways rather than simply maintaining their level of commitment to ending violence against women.

These findings coalesce with other research which has highlighted the crucial role that women in men's personal lives often play in directly or indirectly raising their consciousness and encouraging them to become involved in efforts to end gender-based violence (for example, see Christian, 1994; Guasch, 2012; Burrell, 2019).

Personal experiences of violence and abuse within the family

We were aware when starting this research of the very personal and potentially distressing motivations behind some men's involvement. Previous research into young men's engagement in anti-violence activism has found an overlap with seeing or hearing about violence against women or girls known to them (Coulter, 2003). We made it clear before the interviews that we were open to hearing this information if they felt able to tell us – either as victims, survivors, observers or as men who had themselves used violence or abuse against women or girls. Being explicit that researchers are open to hearing about personal experiences of violence and abuse is also something that is under-studied and under-recognised within research with women in this field. Generally, people are slotted into boxes of being 'experts', 'academics' or 'practitioners' on the one hand or 'survivors' (or indeed 'perpetrators') on the other with little, if any, opportunity to consider how these identities might overlap.

There was certainly this overlap for some of our participants. For one man, there had distinctly been what Casey and Smith (2010) call a key 'sensitising' moment in his childhood, although it wasn't until later in life that he was able to connect this moment to a wider political or academic knowledge base. His 'sensitising moment' came when a family member (relationship not used to maintain anonymity) was subject to an arranged marriage. In this case, the participant overheard his family member talking to other young women, a conversation that was particularly influential and stayed with him until adulthood:

> When I was 10 I went to Pakistan to see my [family member] be married, she had an Islamic marriage but not a British marriage, then the idea was that she would then have an English marriage. But after the Islamic marriage she started saying 'I'm not really happy about this'. And I was listening to the conversations she was having with my other [female family members]. And eventually she did speak up and said she didn't want to be married to him.

[…] So, I would have to say it's my [family member] that influenced me into this. I was 13 years old at the time, I was just a young man, a boy, I didn't have a voice, but I was upset seeing my [family member] was upset, and this influenced me. (Abbas, UK)

Although the 'sensitising moment' in this example is primarily about victimisation, Abbas described how there was simultaneously an experience of family members (parents and extended family) as well as the wider community using abuse in the form of 'emotional blackmail' with the threat of being ostracised. This became complicated once the participant started working in the area of honour-based violence, including forced marriages. He spoke to his parents about it, describing it as a 'touchy subject' that he initially wasn't sure whether he wanted discuss with them: 'it was studying them in a way, you could say that they were the perpetrators albeit if they didn't realise they were perpetrators'. He explained that, as well as publicly speaking out about honour-based violence, he also plays an ongoing role 'consoling' his parents, highlighting that they did eventually intervene and shouldn't feel guilty. Ultimately, it is the female family member, the victim-survivor of the forced marriage, that is less comfortable about the interviewee's work and asks that he does not specifically relate 'her story' to his work in the area. As such, the link between the personal and the professional is (rightly in this instance) hidden within his work despite it being a personally motivating background.

Another UK interviewee recalled an even earlier childhood memory, although as with the previous example it was not until later that he was able to name this as domestic abuse:

I've got a very vivid memory of a very early experience of my parents driving us to a family home, and then, an aunt getting into the car, and she had bruising on her face, and it was only afterwards, that I had the language and frame of reference to understand, that obviously, it was a domestically abusive relationship that she was in. And my parents were going to rescue to her in a way, or help her to get away, and go somewhere safe. (Christopher, UK)

Most of the experiences of men's violence against women that the interviewees talked about were ones that were very close to them. However, one man talked about how he had been influenced not only by seeing violence within the family (in his case his uncle was violent towards his wife), but also by the multiple other 'maybe 30' times he had witnessed violence against women. This might sound shocking on first reading, that one man had witnessed so many acts. However, when we remember that violence against women includes forms such as sexual harassment, it begins to sound not only realistic, but also quite an ordinary or typical amount. This raises the question of how other men in our sample seem to have witnessed or been able to recall so few or no examples, or it may point to different definitions or perceptions about what 'counts' as violence against women.

Grandfathers, fathers, brothers and uncles – male influences when growing up

Many of the men discussed a general lack of positive male figures in their childhoods. This was either because their fathers were absent and their mother had not had another significant relationship with a man during their childhood, or because the men in their family took a particularly 'back seat', 'hands off' or 'strict' approach to them, meaning they were difficult to engage with or seek support from.

In its most extreme form, one of our interviewees described his father as an 'anti-role model – he was everything we refused to become' (Luke, UK). Dag, likewise, had been particularly influenced by a violent uncle and this had shaped what he did not want to become:

> I had an uncle whom I was very afraid of, as [laughter] some kind of inspiration. […] This person has used a lot of violence and I have been subject to it, to his violence, on occasion as a child. But it was through him that I learned to be afraid of men. So, I guess that is some kind of inspiration, in a weird way. But it was not like, that I had anyone else who could show me a way. I didn't have that experience, those came along much, much later. (Dag, Sweden)

Lessons learnt from other boys and men did not tend to be described in positive terms either, and in hindsight left some of our interviewees feeling shame about their earlier years:

> I was obsessed with women and sex, not very successfully I should say. But I thought about it all the time, and I started to see women as sexual objects not as friends. Although I had some women who were friends, the underlying aim was always to have sex. My father, I later found out, was

always having affairs, and he later said that the bane of his life was his sexual desire [...] What I learnt was from my brother or books. I was walking around in the darkness and not knowing what to do about it, I knew this sexual drive was here. I was quite forceful as a teenager with women, in a way that even now makes me shudder. Not in the legal sense – I didn't do anything terrible – but I think it's terrible now and as I look back now I shudder. What gave me the right to do these things? (Bob, UK)

Often, it was only when men moved away from their families that their awareness was awakened or encouraged. For example, one Swedish interviewee described how his childhood had been filled with ostracism both at home and school because of his disability and ethnicity, leaving him determined to leave as soon as possible. This was particularly the case for men who moved from rural to urban areas. As well as the awakening and awareness raising linked to the city and being away from places related to their childhood, there was a newfound confidence linked to the relative anonymity of moving to a city. One Spanish interviewee also discussed how moving from a rural to an urban environment connected with the development of his profeminist consciousness and anti-violence activism:

It would have been much more difficult to do this in the environment I grew up in, but I could do this in the city. When they started, this group of men, there was a perception that they were 'just a bunch of faggots'. But the group of men supported each other, they would meet at the house of one of the men and they would cook, and do this men only, and deconstruct the hegemonic masculinity, and look at what they could do to create challenges. (Didac, Spain)

Similarly, one man in the Swedish cohort found no inspiration in his rural home: it was only when he moved as a young adult to the city and to university that his awareness was encouraged or awakened. However, even where neither parent provided what interviewees saw as strong encouragement or inspiration, they could still play an influential role: for instance, for one Swedish man whose parents encouraged him to show emotions including sadness.

In the minority of cases where a male family member was mentioned as a positive influence, this tended not to be their father. One of our interviewees (Didac) described growing up in a very strict, religious and patriarchal environment in rural Spain, which was more commonplace in Francoist Spain than today. The family was large (he was one of several children) and authoritarian. He contrasted his father's role within the family (the head of the household and breadwinner, who was scarcely involved in childcare which tended to be 'delegated' to female members of the family) with the role that his maternal grandfather took on when his grandmother fell ill (cooking for her, brushing her hair, being involved in childcare). His maternal grandfather was a model of masculinity that he felt more connected to – in direct contrast to his father's. Some other figures in his life also had a positive influence in this respect, such as some of his teachers, as well as other people he learned about through reading and studying; he discussed how concentrating at school, college and university led him towards constructing a different kind of masculine identity.

There were other cases where other men were contrasted positively with their fathers, too. In one case it was a youth leader who supported one of the Swedish interviewees who offered a different model from his violent father and helped him move out of an increasingly criminal lifestyle. However, the idea that boys needed 'good male role models' was one that was challenged by some:

> We never felt a male role model lacking – men don't need male role models and the assumption that they do often just carries the implicit idea that certain characteristics are gendered, which they're not. We learned how to be good human beings simply from observing and aspiring to be like mum and learning to avoid imitating our father. (Luke, UK)

> There's a lot of talk about men being influenced by other men, men being positive role models. It's a bit problematic the idea that men will listen to other men more than to women. But also, do they? Depends what the men are saying! (Dean, UK)

These comments illustrate that role models can be much more complex than is sometimes assumed, and that men can find inspiration from a range of different sources.

Alternative, non-conforming or marginalised masculinities when growing up

One important factor described by several of the interviewees about their pathways was a sense of disquiet and of not fitting in with hegemonic norms of masculinity when growing up. Sometimes this rejection of such norms among the interviewees was overt and for others it was more of a complex relationship with them – for example, subscribing to hegemonic norms while in a group but internally not 'signing up' so fully.

> During my teenage years, I had a strong interest in and quite a lot of awareness in gender, and how it limited boys and girls, men and women, and I felt it limited me a lot. I felt very disaffected about it. That doesn't mean I took much of a public stance. To the extent it did, it would have been with my peer group, mostly with some of my friends who I felt comfortable exploring some of those things with. (Dean, UK)

For some of the participants, this rejection of hegemonic norms was closely associated with being gay. For example, one of the Spanish interviewees pointed to the centrality of his early experiences of growing up gay in his pathway towards starting to speak out against men's violence against women. He drew attention to some serious bullying and violence he experienced as an adolescent, and argued that his gay identity caused him to question habitual (heterosexual) ways of being male:

> Because I am gay, and this kind of makes, I think it makes me more question what is masculinity, because I am not a typical boy, I don't do the typical things and also, it's for some a kind of violence. (Pablo, Spain)

This interviewee explicitly made the link between his own experience and realisation of wider aspects of discrimination: 'For me it is not easy, and I need to make another construction of my identity as a man. And it's for that I think I feel more open about discrimination' (Pablo, Spain). He argued that his gay identity had made him sensitive to discrimination against women; for him, this understanding began in adolescence and was reinforced at university. He had some friends when he was a teenager who were also gay, and they were able to support each other and talk about issues such as these. This account reflects Peretz's finding (2017) that gay men's pathways towards anti-violence are directly influenced by their own life experiences, by understanding their own experiences of violence or marginalisation and placing them in a wider patriarchal social context.

This was also the case for Matthew, one of the UK interviewees, who described his experience of growing up gay as having a significant impact upon his understanding of masculinity and an inherent sense that he was 'different' from other men:

> My perception of men and masculinity is a bit different, and is shaped by being a gay man. My dad is hypermasculine, and my brother has taken that on to some extent too, but I guess I had an awareness from a very young age that my sense of masculinity was quite different. (Matthew, UK)

Matthew, along with other interviewees (discussed further in Chapter 3) felt that gay men were more likely to take a public stance about different issues relating to gender, including men's violence against women. He suggested that growing up with a more critical lens towards dominant notions of masculinity, which might be learnt as a result of experiencing a form of 'subordinated masculinity' as a gay man (Connell, 2005), was one factor that might encourage this.

A critical perspective towards masculinity from a young age was certainly not universal among the interviewees however, and for some it was only later in their lives that they started to question more seriously the gendered expectations placed upon men. For instance, one of the Spanish interviewees, who was also gay, noted that when he was a child he was 'really sensitive to inequality but not gender' (Juan, Spain). As an example, he highlighted how he helped new students from Poland or Russia who didn't know Spanish, both with language and with understanding an unfamiliar education system. In particular, he pointed to his strong relationship with his grandmother as especially important to him; she had Alzheimer's disease, 'so I had to take care of her, bring her to the, like the doctor, to the care home, because my mum used to work' (Juan, Spain). Taking his grandmother to the care home and picking her up continued while he was studying for his Master's degree. This again points to the role that close relationships with women, together with taking on caring responsibilities, can factor in encouraging men to question rigid constraints of masculinity, and potentially in turn helping them to speak out against the oppression of women.

For some of the men, it was holding a privileged status rather than a marginalised one that opened up spaces for them to step outside of traditional male gender norms. For instance, a Swedish interviewee described his middle-class family background playing an important role in him not seeking the company of, or being dependent on, men in groups:

I've always had the space to back off. And that has meant me never being into these, I haven't been… a little bit outside of the kind of hard groups of guys. I have never belonged to a group of lads. And my own theory is that I simply have… […] I have a little bit of a side view at it. I have definitely – sometimes I've been in, and sometimes [out]. I think it has something to do with my class background too, making me. I've also had the self-confidence, in some kind of way, to sometimes take part in [groups of men/boys]. But then I also have had the confidence to step out. (Kristian, Sweden)

Finally, not being 'sporty', particularly in terms of traditional boys' team sports such as football, was for some participants the way they had started to feel different to other boys. One recalled his time within a boys-only state grammar school and feeling frustrated about the attention that sport was given:

There was quite a lot of emphasis on sport. I wasn't much good at it, or very interested in most sports, but it certainly got you a lot of kudos among the boys and the school. I was very academic and got a certain amount of kudos from the school, but not, as you can imagine, from the other boys – it certainly didn't make you cool. People might have been impressed, but it didn't help your social relationships very much, and wasn't really encouraged in your peer group. So, I was ploughing my own furrow to some extent. I was a bit pissed off with the focus on sport and did as little of it as I could get away with. (Dean, UK)

Others started off attempting to fit into traditional norms. As a child, Dag originally chose football as a way of avoiding violence and conforming with gender norms. However, when moving to a larger city, taking up studies and starting to challenge norms of masculinity, he was later regarded as 'the lost son' from time to time by members of his family in a way that expresses how he became different from other family members:

Yes, from my family I could hear that 'Oh, it's great that you work with these things'. But my feeling has from time to time been that – especially when I started to challenge gender norms – that 'Well, it's Dag, the lost son who moved to the city' […] being understood as behaving somewhat remarkable and superior, and doing a lot of strange stuff. Not that it is put in words, more the feeling of it. Like, the lost son. (Dag, Sweden)

However, Dag describes his siblings as supportive of him being non-conforming in his way of doing masculinity, that they have been curious and expressing that they get to know another side of him.

Becoming a father

Casey and Smith's (2010) study found that having children was a significant driving force for some of the men in their research – prompting them to reflect on the world that they would be raising them in. In our sample, it was not always that having children was the specific catalyst, but rather that having children was linked to a general 'growing up' or sense of becoming more mature. For one man having children had awakened him to many more forms of sexism in his private life, but not specifically to violence:

> I had children very young so I made a decision that I didn't like what was placed on young men, and particularly men as fathers for example, so we did childcare very differently etc. but it was in my private life. Again, sexism yes, but violence against women no. (James, UK)

For one of the interviewees who had been influenced by witnessing violence from his uncle to his aunt as well as by other men against women, he recalls a key 'sensitising moment' as being one occasion when he was out with his daughter and witnessed a man being violent to a woman:

> Seeing someone next to my house, bringing out their girlfriend and pulling her along by the leg on the streets, and my daughter hearing that and feeling that she was herself beaten by that violence, and I have to get involved. (Jon, Spain)

We also had a number of examples of men involved in anti-sexism work taking action on fatherhood as a dual or secondary topic linked to their anti-violence against women work. This is the case for some organisations as well, such as MÄN in Sweden, which campaigns on both fatherhood and on violence against women, particularly sexual violence. This was also the case for some UK interviewees who were involved in setting up crèches (childcare facilities) to enable women in the Women's Liberation Movement to attend conferences and other actions. Likewise, in Spain there were men who were active around both issues too:

> During this day [21 October] we go to the streets in Barcelona and not only Barcelona, in many Spanish cities and villages. We make some kind of marches in the street, and vigils of men, because there is a specific section in society of men against violence against women. And the other campaign is, so 19th of March is the Day of the Father in Spain, and we make some actions in the street also. With these actions in these areas we make visible these issues. One is violence and the other is paternity – and our call for a different type of paternity. (Pablo, Spain)

It was agreed at the Ibero-American Congress on Masculinities and Equality (CIME) in 2011 to celebrate two public actions by men: 21 October against violence against women, and 19 March to promote a more egalitarian form of fatherhood. Becoming a father could also spark off more everyday reflections about gender inequalities and how they manifest themselves within one's personal life, which men might not otherwise consider. For instance, Lucas commented:

> We choose to see certain things and not. Just the other day, my daughter said: 'But Dad, you say that you can wear everything, why don't you have a skirt?' (Lucas, Sweden)

This exemplifies how ordinary things which are often taken for granted can tell a lot about gender norms and expectations, and being a father (perhaps especially of girls) can provide important insights into this for men.

Men and boys' violence against other men and boys

It was the violence and aggression that our participants had experienced at the hands of other men and boys that was a motivating factor for some, for instance, the violence of male family members. One interviewee talked about contrasting the gentleness and kindness of his older brother as opposed to the violence he experienced from his father, for example. Similarly, one Swedish participant whose father was violent in the home contrasted this behaviour with his father's more caring older brother, who provided another model of how a man could be. Another talked about the impact of being sexually abused as a child by a man. Several participants also discussed the effects of witnessing and experiencing acts of violence by men in society more broadly, whether that be from their peers, figures of authority such as sports coaches, or men in public spaces, and how this motivated them to choose to behave differently.

For Kristian, one of the Swedish interviewees, witnessing violence by men and boys when growing up, for example at school, had a significant impact on him, and meant that the idea of men being violent towards women didn't seem atypical:

> One very evident thing for me is that, as a child, it was always the men I was afraid of. I was never afraid of women. Even though I have been in situations when women have been frightening as well, it was as if I had a rather clear picture, wherever that comes from. My point of view was that if there is someone who is dangerous it's men […] You know, that sort of stuff never happens with girls, I mean girls towards me, rather it was always boys. So, I think for me the idea of men's violence [against women] was very reasonable. Like, yeah [laughter] I know lots about that. (Kristian, Sweden)

Instead, Kristian described the idea and knowledge of men using violence against women as already being established 'within him', as being part of himself.

Childhood bullying at school, most often by other boys, but also occasionally by girls, is a common theme that runs throughout our data. In many cases this was because the participant was seen as being 'different' in some way to their peers. There were multiple examples given of abuse being related to disability, ethnicity and, in particular, sexuality. This highlights how gender can intersect with other systems of power and inequality; men who are not white, able-bodied and heterosexual, for example, may be perceived as failing to meet the hegemonic ideal of masculinity, and may be bullied and ostracised as a result. It's also important to remember that gendered identities are not only formed at home, and masculine norms are not only observed from and enforced by individuals. Social institutions such as schools are key sites for learning about violence, including through the aggressive ways in which boys often relate to each other, codes of toughness and the use of violence as part of masculine identification and social status, and the often commonplace taken-for-granted nature of fights among boys at school.

For one of the Spanish interviewees, the death of his father meant moving from a town to a small village. He recalled what he called the 'masculine rituals' that he was put through almost immediately after moving, including having to physically fight boys who held influence within peer groups and start smoking cigarettes:

> I managed to perform well in all those fields, but the costs were terrible. It's thinking that you are able to do anything, that you do not need to know anyone, that you can take the responsibility of everything. (Jon, Spain)

In contrast, for one of the UK interviewees, it was taking a stance against violence witnessed among boys on the school playground that he recalled as being when he first took some form of action against violence:

> I can remember when I was at primary school questioning and challenging boys who were fighting with other boys. And saying 'why do you do that?' and 'that's not a good idea'. So, it was anti-violence but not anti-violence against women. (Dean, UK)

One of the Swedish interviewees described how he would avoid spending time with other boys when growing up, such as by not taking part in sports, in order to try and keep away from the violence which often pervaded interactions between them:

> My background in school was that I was never with guys, because I thought it was difficult with them, it was hard. Avoid sports… there was an issue here that has to do with gender. It was a lot of violence growing up there in the countryside, a lot of violence that I, myself was exposed to from other guys as well. So, it's not really strange that you suddenly become interested [in gender issues]; 'Oh, look here, it says something'. (Jack, Sweden)

The above quotes exemplify that the men used different strategies for coping with violence in their youth, ranging from involvement, to resistance, to avoidance.

Influences at university

For the men who were university educated, higher education emerged as a key space in which they were able to start to make sense of and/or become politicised about gender and other inequalities they had seen or experienced when growing up.

For some men, this was because they specifically chose a social sciences course which sometimes included some form of feminist content, gender studies modules or lectures. Often this was linked to a general political awakening through involvement in student groups and the politics of others within friendship groups or house shares.

This general political awakening linking gender inequality and, in time, violence against women to the development of their broader political standpoints and social consciousness was seen across our sample. For example, for one of our Spanish interviewees, leaving home and going to university was an escape from the authoritarian rural household he had grown up in. His response to his patriarchal upbringing was to choose to study sociology, which at the time was considered a subversive choice. He shared houses with other students, joined political student groups and became a left-wing activist. In his interview with us he reflected upon the influence of Marxist thought on his development and how gender equality fitted into that ideology. In his student activism, he felt it important to fight against both class and gender-based inequalities.

A similar situation is recalled by one of the UK interviewees, Dean, who had started out intervening in playground violence between boys, then moved into being concerned with sexist attitudes in his teenage years but not particularly feeling able to call it out beyond his immediate peer group. This changed once he had both the freedom that higher education brought him but also the access to feminist knowledge and also more politically connected peers:

> When I was at university, I got a bit more public about it. I became more aware of a feminist approach, looking at the specific ways women were disadvantaged. That included sexual violence, gender violence. I was reading about it a lot, talking to an increasing number of people. I helped organise a number of peer-led talks for men run by myself and other undergraduates at Oxford about various related issues. (Dean, UK)

For those who became active in the 1970s and 1980s at university, it was feminist women who were part of the emerging Women's

Liberation Movement that influenced them primarily – sometimes as friends and sometimes as partners in intimate relationships. It was often these personal influences that came first, before men started reading and learning more about the topic for themselves:

> I'd love to say I was out on the barricades or challenging my pals on the football team at the age of 17, but I can't remember a single incident before I left home, that I specifically challenged anyone on violence against women. At university in the late 70s I was part of the boys against sexism crowd and some of my friends and my girlfriend at the time were very engaged in Reclaim the Night marches so I was right on the edge of it, and I'd like to think that was how I approached relationships and recognised the advantages I had as a boy – I'd like to think I was open minded, but I think I was learning rather than challenging. (James, UK)

This dynamic also applied to some of the interviewees who went to university more recently. Dag saw his female partner and their very long-lasting relationship as key in leading him to take a public stance. She always pushed him and asked provoking questions, and encouraged him to engage in gender studies at the university. But these studies were intertwined with random opportunities and coincidences:

> I wrote [gender studies in application] as a third-hand option when I applied and I didn't have enough good grades for the first two. And then, we could take the course together. I had no idea what I was getting into (laughs). So, I wish there had been a conscious strive, but it was more the coincidences combined with a partner saying 'this is important for you, it will do you good'. (Dag, Sweden)

The process towards coming to work with issues of anti-violence is emphasised in this narrative, where university studies were complemented with education in violence prevention and meeting women's shelter movement activists. However, university studies themselves did not necessarily have to be what initiated their involvement or awakening. Lucas reported:

> I didn't do politics or was involved in societal issues – I did pretty classic [male], sports. I became involved in that

primarily when I was admitted to a course at the Swedish Association for Sexuality Education (RFSU), and started to read more and discuss issues in a more structured way around theories. Since then I have changed and made a journey from some kind of essentialist feminist to some kind of constructionist feminist and maybe queer feminism during this period. But this actually happened at the same time as I started studying at the university. (Lucas, Sweden)

Meanwhile, for Kristian, his public stance in his personal life and as an activist started with meeting a woman who was involved in a network of feminists and anti-racists. The friendship evolved into a relationship. His conversations with this person were described as his 'political awakening'. Getting involved in this network made him switch careers after a few years from a university degree occupation to reading feminist theory on his own. He then dedicated his working life to issues of gendered violence.

For Iain, who has been involved in the UK violence against women movement for 40 years, he also first came to the topic through anti-sexist men's groups – particularly Crèches against Sexism and Vasectomies against Sexism. He described a gradual process whereby he had lived in all-feminist collective households and had intimate relationships with feminist women, and that it was from this that his education came: 'hanging out with feminist women has a massive impact on men' (Iain, UK).

A few men, for example Juan from Spain, had specifically taken modules or courses at university and had gained a clear interest from this point. However, in some cases, although university had been a space to learn about violence against women, it was not until they entered the workplace that they were able to apply this and really understand its importance. A number of men talked about the way in which their learning at university started to connect and became more 'felt' later in their life:

> Before, I had read about it. But now it started to 'come down', into my body; the consequences of men's violence to other people. I had studied and understood, but now it went from the head into my stomach. (Dag, Sweden)

The quote is interesting in the way knowledge (from education and literature) is transformed into a more personal understanding in a way that it becomes interwoven with the self. 'Feeling' what he knows not just intellectually, but also in 'the stomach', hereby resembling more of a form of experiential knowledge located in the body.

Being influenced by a specific, high profile case of men's violence against women

In some cases, especially in Spain, participants described being influenced by particularly notorious cases that received a high degree of media and public attention. While this did not necessarily act as a specific trigger for the men we interviewed to realise the extent of gender based inequalities, these cases did seem to have an influence on men who were already engaged in the anti-sexist men's movement in that they tuned them more acutely into the specific issue of men's violence against women and the role that an anti-sexist men's movement might play in ending it.

One such case was that of Ana Orantes from Granada, Spain in 1997. Ana Orantes appeared on a Spanish television programme talking about the lifelong domestic abuse that she had suffered (she was aged 60 at the time of the interview). Two weeks after the television programme was aired, Ana was set on fire and killed by her ex-husband on the patio of their home. This awakened a general anger and increased understanding of the link between sexism, gender and violence against women in Spain. One of our interviewees explained that before Ana's case was publicised, crimes of men killing intimate partners tended to be talked about as 'crimes of passion' rather than crimes related to gender violence, and as 'private matters' to be managed and solved inside the family, rather than a public concern.

Ana had only recently been able to divorce her husband, and the judge forced them to share the same house (with one living upstairs and the other downstairs). This was despite the fact that she had on 15 occasions reported to the police acts of physical violence and abuse by her ex-husband, and had repeatedly sought help from different services. The murder, its brutality and the social impact it had through the media coverage, combined with the fact that she had been so massively failed by the different institutions of society, were a trigger for a significant change in public opinion, and for the introduction of one of the first European Laws against gender-based violence in Spain in 2004. This was followed by other important Spanish legislation on gender equality in subsequent years, too. It also led to an upsurge in anti-violence activism among some men:

> There was some form of breakthrough and epiphany with a group of men, and they decided to create the

'Men's Group of Sevilla' created in 1997 – the same year
Ana Orantes was killed – which had as its main focus to
challenge patriarchy. They published a manifesto, *The
Silence of the Accomplices*, and had much more support than
they thought, and they were surprised how much support
there was from Latin America, and they started doing men
only demonstrations against violence against women and
patriarchy. (Didac, Spain)

There was an element of celebrity support here too, from the famous
Portuguese writer Jose Saramago, who wrote about this case and the
issue of men's violence.

There are similar cases in Sweden such as the honour-based killings
of Pela Atroshi in 1999 and Fadime Sahindal in 2002 which received
a lot of media coverage at the time, and the founding of a national
organisation GAPF (in English, Never Forget Pela and Fadime),
supporting women and working with agencies and political parties
against honour-based violence and murders of women, girls and
boys. However, Pela and Fadime were not brought up specifically
by interviewees in the study as cases giving a specific focus for men
to engage in the same way as for Spanish participants. Likewise, in
the UK sample there were examples of personal tragedy influencing
men but not a specific case at a national level that was some kind of
'turning point'.

Being 'catapulted' into the work due to a personal tragedy

This theme has overlaps with the two previous sections on personal
experiences of violence and abuse and that of being influenced by a
specific, high profile case of violence. It stands on its own as a specific
theme too, however, as for these men it was not part of a process of
involvement as it was for others – it was a shocking, life changing,
moment of realisation and a sudden and unexpected catapulting into
the world of anti-violence against women work. While this theme has
not been specifically identified in previous research, it was identified as a
theme within two of the three countries we studied and we hypothesise
that it is an emerging way that men are beginning to speak out. We
are not aware of similar cases at the moment in Sweden, but this is not
to say that they do not exist.

We were aware of this becoming important in Spain because so
many interviewees spoke of being influenced by the killing of Ana

Orantes. The case was already one that had received a high level of public attention because Ana had been interviewed on television a few weeks before she was murdered stating her fear of being killed. Her prediction and fear in advance of her murder bursts the myth somewhat of men's killing of women being unpredictable acts of passion that cannot be prevented. However, another reason that this case became such a significant turning point, covered so extensively in the media, was because of the involvement of her son, Fran Orantes, in speaking out about his mother's murder in the media. He also subsequently wrote a chapter within a book on 'Men for Gender Equality' (Coronado, 2017), entitled 'A mother is forever' (Orantes, 2017).

In the UK, we were personally aware of four men who had spoken out publicly and consistently following personal tragedies. We conducted two interviews relating to three of these four men (with one interviewee representing himself and his brother) within our UK interview sample.

The first man we interviewed who was 'catapulted' in had been working in a senior role within financial services, before that as an accountant, when his life changed instantly and dramatically. His sister and nephew were murdered by his brother in law – his nephew's father – in 2003. Our interviewee (though we do not name him within this book, he is aware that he may be identified as his details are so specific) started to speak out publicly not because of the deaths themselves but because of the actions of the police both before and after the murders. He started speaking out publicly in the media about the failings he and his family had identified, then going on to author his own newspaper articles, and eventually to become the coordinator of a charity. The charity provides expert and specialist advocacy to raise the status of families bereaved through domestic homicides and to train professionals including domestic homicide chairs (in the UK, every domestic homicide is required by statute to have a review). In his interview, he explained the motivation for becoming involved:

> Well our sister and my nephew were murdered, and we couldn't stop it. And we tried to stop it, but we were ignorant about how to prevent it. And we didn't know better. And we were ignored by the police. And we used the public protection system that we were told to use, and this system was found wanting [...] We felt we wanted the truth to come out, and to know what the police did with the information we gave them, and we wanted to see their firearms policy, and we wanted to see some progress on

improvements. We weren't looking for blame but to achieve justice for our family – there's nothing worse than the smell of bullshit after something like this has happened. (Lee, UK)

For this participant, it wasn't predominantly the personal tragedy and devastation caused to his family by the murderer that led him to becoming an activist – it was about the failures of people, organisations and systems that they previously had trust in. In his words:

> I was very, very driven. We had an unsatisfactory inquest, my bother-in-law said 'what is obvious is something is broken and we don't think we can walk away until it is fixed'. So, we know that the police response was very poor, no strategic leadership, and we wanted some way to expose that and then fix it. So, we weren't looking for heads on a plate – we wanted a true story told and we wanted to see change, and I was very driven about that. (Lee, UK)

For this participant, there wasn't anything particular in his childhood or adolescence that related to his becoming involved. He saw his childhood as a happy one, one of eight children in a catholic family; he described his father as traditional and having to work hard to support the children, but being open minded with it. Neither he nor his siblings had any level of formal or informal education in terms of feminism.

Similarly, for the other participant who suffered a personal tragedy, there was no prior education or specific interest in feminism, however their childhood was not a happy one. This participant interviewed on behalf of their brother as well as themselves. Again, these interviewees are aware they may be identified by their interview data as their experience is so particular – especially because they are brothers, are constantly in the public eye and because they have written a book about their experience. In the UK, the fact that they are brothers speaking out in a profeminist way about men's violence against women is enough for most people working within the movement to identity them. For this reason, and at their request, we use their real first names in our book and also cite from their book.

In July 2016, news channels and newspapers in the UK ran a 'breaking news' story, with a rolling commentary and helicopter footage showing that a man had used a shotgun to shoot two people, and then himself, in a swimming pool car park in Spalding, England. Once the case was deemed a domestic homicide and not a terrorist incident in which general members of the public were at risk, the rolling news reporting stopped – as is often the case when it comes to news coverage of domestic homicides. This case, though – where our interviewees' mother Claire and 19-year-old sister Charlotte were killed by their father – has remained in the public eye because of their commitment to raising awareness of coercive control.

Their book details, to a greater extent than we are able to cover, what happened before and after the murders and we recommend this book for further reading (Hart and Hart, 2018). For this study, we asked them to recall the first time they decided to speak out publicly:

> About nine months after the murders, aged 25 and 26 respectively, Ryan and I first spoke to Victoria Derbyshire on the BBC to highlight the rampant apologism we saw in the media (and among locals) for our father's murders. It felt as if our father had not gone when we saw many media outlets and onlookers saying precisely what our father would have said. That was when we realised this was not an isolated family tragedy. This was the societally-condoned murder of insubordinate women. (Luke, UK)

For Luke and Ryan, their reasons for speaking out publicly are three-fold but linked. First, it is about keeping the memory of their mother and sister alive; Luke told us this is why they wrote their book 'Remembered Forever', 'to memorialise Mum and Charlotte'. Secondly, it is to raise awareness and create important social change:

> … to address the social causes of domestic homicides and advocate for much more to be done to end not only the vast indifference to the deaths of women and children in our society, but also to hold to account those who sympathise, excuse or even reinforce these murderers. (Luke, UK)

Thirdly, Luke describes the process of speaking out as empowering for them, as men who grew up under the tight grasp of coercive control and entrapped by a poverty their father created to maintain dominance over the family:

> We have found speaking incredibly empowering, in fact after the murders is the first time we were ever taken seriously. Often, when people speak about coercive control they are trivialised or badly misunderstood by others. Unfortunately, it often takes a tragedy before anyone is

willing to accept your how bad things may have been [...]
We always strived to make Mum and Charlotte proud, and
we want to make sure that we create a legacy for them that
would honour them. (Luke, UK)

Employment/professional involvement

Our interviews found that professional influences are also providing an
increasingly important route through which more men are developing
an awareness of and vocal opposition to men's violence against women.
It is possible that more men are coming into contact with these issues in
their professional lives, as institutions and services in different European
countries have gradually started to take different forms of violence
against women more seriously in recent decades as a result of pressure
from feminist movements. This finding is in line with the argument
made by Messner, Greenberg and Peretz (2015) that 'professional
pathways' are becoming increasingly significant in shaping men's routes
towards anti-violence work. For example, just over half of our survey
respondents (58 per cent) were involved in some form of paid work
as part of their stance against violence against women.

Some men get involved in paid work in this area after becoming
committed to taking action against men's violence towards women.
However, for others it is while doing the jobs they already do that
they come to understand and take on this commitment. Sometimes
men had become involved in events that they now felt were not the
most appropriate type of action. For example, one man (Robert) in
our UK sample had participated in a 'heel walk' as part of his work
linked to a city council. 'Heel walks' were a relatively common
occurrence in the UK in the 2010s, and still are to a lesser degree. In
these walks, men (typically middle class, middle aged white men in
grey suits) were encouraged to walk down a public part of the town
or city wearing a pair of women's very high heeled shoes with the
idea that this represented walking in women's shoes, and having some
kind of empathy and understanding of what it means to be a woman.
There have been many criticisms of this approach as a way of speaking
out against men's violence against women (for example, see Bridges,
2010), not least the stereotyping of women wearing very high heels.
As Robert's first formal experience of taking a public stance through
a work-based activity, it left him feeling disappointed and trying to
find some better ways of taking action.

Even more closely linked to work as a route to becoming involved
was when men were 'allocated' the domestic abuse or violence against

women portfolio as part of their paid work. This was the case for Bob from our UK sample, who was working within the police when he was asked to become the lead and attend partnership meetings about domestic abuse. While for some of the men it was gender inequality awareness that developed first and the interest or attention on violence against women came second, the men who entered through a work-based route tended to first take an interest in violence against women and the gender inequality understanding came later. This was particularly the case for the Spanish interviewees but also for some of the UK men who became involved while at university or while involved in left wing politics. This was how Bob first came to be involved:

> I didn't talk much about gender equality at the time because I didn't really grasp the issues and wasn't really politically conscious. I could do something about domestic violence as I was responsible for it, but gender equality was a bit more vague in my response. (Bob, UK)

Over time though, Bob came to realise that gender and other intersecting inequalities were at the root of men's violence against women. He described how this newfound realisation had a massive impact on him that reverberated through his personal and professional life. Having previously treated women as 'sexual objects' and being 'quite forceful as a teenager with women, in a way that even now makes me shudder', he described himself after this realisation as 'poacher turned gamekeeper':

> I became almost fanatical. My brother who is older than me, he's had a different life and he hasn't had to think about this, so he would send me sexist and racist jokes on the phone just to wind me up. You know if over the Christmas meal someone would say something, like my mother the other day said something that identified them as a homosexual, and I said but he also has two ears, why identify him as a homosexual? And she's 94. So I've calmed down a little. But I've got myself into real trouble with it. (Bob, UK)

Such experiences challenge the assumption that men involved in activism against men's violence towards women will typically arrive at that point via a pre-existing awareness about and support of feminism.

This was also the case for Pedro, who first became involved through a work-based route. He described:

> The first contact and awareness with gender violence was as a forensic doctor. And on the other hand, I was also used to seeing victims. Of course, it was not a huge surprise to meet or see a woman with violence, was it? But it is true that most of the victims were men who fought – fights. The usual were weekend fights, in a pub, in sports activities, neighbourhood problems etc. But when I started seeing abused women, at that time it was 1988… they came with serious, serious injuries. Because the level of consciousness, the level of criticism required more violence to report, to file a complaint, because it required going to court, and it required more violence and then it was already a formal complaint […] That idea of 'normality in violence' is what struck me, and then I started to work, to investigate. And then I began to speak in public, at conferences, about this reality, about this violence. (Pedro, Spain)

Pedro pointed out that this served as a driving force for his involvement – the systematic rejection he experienced from his male colleagues who perceived the study of gender-based violence as being something unimportant, as 'women's things' (Pedro, Spain).

Summary

In line with previous research in this area, our findings across the three locations show that most men went through a gradual process of becoming involved in taking a public stance against violence towards women. The exceptions here were when men became 'catapulted' in when one or more family members were murdered by a man within the family. Most often it was a general awareness and activism around anti-sexism that came first, sometimes alongside an increasing involvement in other social movements and left-wing politics. The exception to this was some professional routes in, where their awareness of men's violence against women came before an awareness of and commitment to anti-sexism.

Largely negative experiences in relation to other men and boys when growing up was the norm for most of our interviewees. This was sometimes because men had not felt that they fitted in with other men and boys while growing up, generally either because of their lack of enjoyment of sport and other traditionally masculine activities or because of being gay. That is not to say that there were not some positive experiences with men, rather that these were in the distinct minority for the men in our sample. Women, either as powerful figures, influential within the family (often referred to by our interviewees as 'strong women'), as friends, within political movements, as teachers and lecturers or as intimate partners, emerged as far more influential in terms of shaping the lives of the men within our research and their pathways towards anti-violence work.

3

Being involved

Having looked at the routes into involvement, we now turn to the experiences of men once they are involved in men's activism to end violence against women. We look at the ways in which men are supported to do this work – primarily through women feminist activists and practitioners – but also to a lesser extent from other men in a range of settings (as friends, as other men working to end violence against women). As well as considering the support and the positive aspects of involvement, it is also important to make visible and discuss the obstacles or struggles that men might face and any problems or limitations of men being involved in this work. Obstacles and struggles can be located in the personal, the professional and/or the political. Even though we at times try to separate these analytically in the book, these spaces, in reality, often overlap. Often, the interviewees described criticisms as coming from multiple directions, from women and women's groups as well as from other men and men's groups.

Women in the movement supporting men to be involved

Just as women emerged as very important in men becoming involved in this work, they were the primary support that men talked about as important to sustaining their involvement. Many of the men we interviewed talked about extremely influential relationships with women that they had longstanding friendships with. In the previous chapter we talked about how women as friends or family were very influential in becoming involved. This part of the chapter is about developing and sustaining that involvement; the focus shifts away from friends and family generally and towards women working in the feminist violence against women movement. These women tended to be described as people who 'pushed', encouraged or provided 'friendly challenge' to the men to develop their thinking and behaviour as male allies to the violence against women movement. In a number of cases the friends were lesbian women working in the movement. One of the Swedish participants highlighted the fact that some of the women who both supported and challenged him were lesbian, describing it as 'refreshing' in both the tone and level of challenge they directed towards him:

> I think also that they weren't heterosexual, they were not interested in any way – I mean, there was not any type of that game going on. They were like, 'Come on mate, this is bollocks'... they didn't feel that they should be gratified by men, so they didn't shun from being critical or even acidic at times. And that was kind of refreshing, you know. (Noah, Sweden)

As a man from a minoritised ethnic background in mainstream Swedish society which he regarded as deeply racist, he commented that it was refreshing to be criticised for something more 'deserved' than the racist attitudes he faced so often:

> Some of my closest friends, and have been for almost 20 years now, happen to be, well, lesbians and feminists. And they would almost self-identify as 'man-hating'. But for me it was like a welcome shift, that somebody – well, they didn't hate me, but they would criticise me. Not because, 'Oh, you, darkie, this is how we do it in this country, learn our ways and behave'. Instead, they said, 'That's so typically male of you'. If they criticized me like that, that felt loyal to me, that criticism, rather than an undeserved criticism. And I was like, 'Okay, I get you, I relate, thanks'. (Noah, Sweden)

Men described a variety of ways in which they received support from women in the violence against women movement. Not surprisingly, this support often worked well when it was reciprocal in nature. One of the interviewees described the work that he did with women's organisations in Northern Ireland:

> Both when I was in practice, in terms of working with the local Women's Aid group, with the families that we were working with and trying to access resources. Later on, in terms of working groups, in terms of developing strategies and policy. And as I moved into academia, in relation to, you know being prepared to co-teach, and also with research projects. And if there was an idea I had for research project and asked them if they would assist, or vice versa, if there was something they wanted to know about, and coming

and asking myself and colleagues if we would assist them with that. So there's been really strong relationships with people in practice. (Christopher, UK)

As well as traditional friendships, online support from feminist activists on social media and online and face to face support from specialist women's organisations was also important. In Spain, having supportive feminist journalists being willing to promote the work the men were doing was important, and this was particularly the case for left-wing media and publications. For example, journalist Nuria Coronado interviewed a series of men in the gender equality arena about their work. This support from activists and feminist professionals and practitioners was mentioned as a significant form of encouragement by participants in interviews across all three countries. Although, as we will also describe later in this chapter, there were also challenges and perceived limitations in terms of these relationships. This support is particularly visible when it comes to social media platforms, predominantly Twitter, where some of the men had their high 'rock star status' both echoed and accentuated within social media.

Interviewees also described private support received from a range of organisations. This was particularly mentioned in the Spanish and UK interviews:

Privately we received many recognitions from the Ministry or from women's associations of every kind, encouraging us. (Jon, Spain)

When I wrote my first book [on violence against women], feminist women, who I was beginning to know then and who have become great friends now, they gave me enormous support. That a man wrote a book about these things that seemed good, they wondered, where did this guy come from? At that time it was not normal at all. (Pedro, Spain)

I went to Southall Black Sisters, I said 'I'm not Black and I'm not one of the Sisters, but can you help?' I told them my work skills. And they said, 'forget all that crap Lee, what you will need more than anything is persistence'. (Lee, UK)

This is not to suggest that men were universally welcomed and supported with open arms into this work. For many, their relationships with some women's organisations were much more complicated and often built upon foundations of mistrust.

Rocky relationships – tensions with women's groups

Feminist and profeminist scholars and activists have highlighted how there are a number of risks associated with men playing a greater role in efforts to end violence against women (for example, see Marchese, 2008; Pease, 2008; Macomber, 2018; Burrell, 2020). This is in particular due to the power and privileges that men receive through patriarchy (and, by extension, the perpetuation of men's violence against women), and the ways in which they may be invested in and benefit from gender inequality and dominant ideas of masculinity as a result. There are a number of ways in which these power dynamics risk being reproduced if the presence of men increases within feminist movements led by women and based around the experiences and injustices they suffer. Given this and the unequal power and privilege that different men hold, it is not surprising that men's relationships with women's groups were not uniformly positive in any of the countries we studied.

In our survey, we asked men about the possible risks of more men taking a public stance on violence against women. The respondents' views on each of these factors were quite mixed, demonstrating the complex and contentious nature of the dangers associated with men's activism to end violence against women. One of the risks we included in the survey was 'increased conflict between women's groups and men's groups'. In fact, this was the risk out of the six we identified that the respondents were least likely to agree with. Just over a quarter (28 per cent) agreed with this statement and the remaining three quarters didn't know, disagreed or strongly disagreed with this statement. There were no respondents at all that strongly agreed.

While in one sense it might be seen as positive that so many respondents did not see this as a risk, it is possible that some were seeing things through 'rose tinted glasses' and being overly optimistic about the challenges. For example, 38 per cent agreed or strongly agreed that 'men diverting money from initiatives to support women' was a risk, and 47 per cent agreed that 'male activists not behaving in non-violent and gender-equal ways' was a risk. It therefore seems contradictory that there would *not* be increased conflict between women's groups and men's groups. Respondents may have therefore found in their own work that these issues were less likely to arise in practice, or had perhaps found ways of overcoming them. It may be

Figure 2: Possible risks of more men taking a public stance on violence against women, n = 40

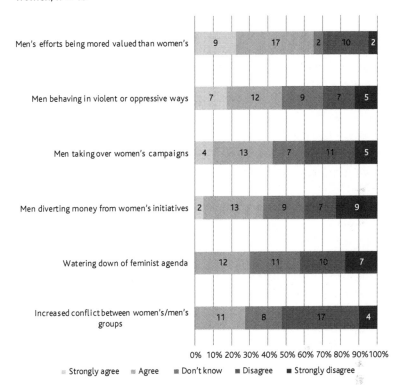

the case that there is a need for men to be more reflective in their day-to-day work about the range of risks than can come about as a result of men's involvement. This could also be concerning in that it may suggest than in some cases, men are not giving sufficient attention to the consequences of their activism on the broader feminist violence against women movement to be able to know the answers to these questions – or perhaps to have enough awareness of the risks that their involvement can create.

In the interviews we were able to explore these issues in greater depth. One quote from a Spanish interviewee summarised the relationship between feminist women's groups and profeminist men's groups as 'good relations, but not close relations' (Pablo, Spain). This working 'side by side', in 'parallel', rather than necessarily 'together' is a good way of summarising what we found across the board. However, there were also examples of far more rocky relationships. There was a tendency by some interviewees to categorise 'groups' or 'sections' of the feminist violence against women movement; with some such groups or organisations seen as more likely than others to accept the idea that there was space for men to be involved. Some doubted there were any benefits at all to men engaging in this work. The following two quotes show examples of this, whereby Jon differentiates between 'a section' of the movement versus the rest, and Abbas differentiates between the women's organisation he is a trustee of versus other women's organisations.

> There has been a section of the feminist movement who have supported us and say 'go on, stand with us', and so on. (Jon, Spain)

> The women's organisation I am a trustee of, they want me to get involved, so they've been quite supportive in that respect. (Abbas, UK)

As with some of the survey responses, in such instances (and this was only the case with a minority of the interviewees) there appeared to be relatively little critical awareness expressed about the dangers that could accompany this approach, such as the potential for men to take over feminist spaces and diminish women's voices and leadership within them. This was also found in Wright's (2009) UK study, which found that male allies would agree with feminist movements 'up to a certain point' or that they could be less supportive of those they saw as 'radical' or extreme'. This was reported to be less often the case in Sweden, where more time seemed to be spent within NGOs on critical awareness than in Spain and the UK. This might reflect national differences in how feminist movement and gender equality politics involving men have been interconnected in the Swedish case (Florin and Nilsson, 2000; Holli et al, 2005; Hearn et al, 2012). In fact, previous research on profeminist men in Sweden suggests that criticism and suspicion from women's groups and the feminist movement is both anticipated and preferred by men, a cautionary position towards other men that profeminist men shared (Egeberg Holmgren, 2007, 2011; Egeberg Holmgren and Hearn 2009).

Some of the Spanish interviewees mentioned that for a long time there was an attitude of suspicion and distrust towards men's groups, in particular from the 'state feminism' of the Institute for Women, with the concern that that they were 'taking over' their space. However, participants felt that since the 2000s men's anti-violence groups have gradually won the respect and support of the women's movement, through practice and time, and by demonstrating that they take accountability seriously. This has also varied with different feminist groups; for example, it was noted that feminists in the academy have generally been more open towards men working in this area.

In a small number of cases, interviewees had expectations of women's groups that were unrealistic. For example, one UK participant talked about some women's organisations being unreceptive to men and giving as an example a time that he invited a women's group by email to work with him on a project he was running. In his interview he talked about feeling disappointed that the organisation had not even taken the time to reply to him. He explained the lack of reply as being because he was a man working in the area of violence against women and that the women's organisation would not want to work with him on the basis of his sex. However, the women's organisation in question is under-resourced, over-worked with serious life-threatening cases of male violence, and it is likely that many researchers' emails go unanswered regardless of the sex of the researcher. In this example, it felt as though either the interviewee had expected a certain 'pedestal' status as a man that they did not receive, or they did not understand the pressures faced by frontline women's organisations and in particular the many requests they get from students and researchers that can threaten to overwhelm their services at times.

Some of the Spanish interviewees also pointed to some difficulties they had experienced in working with or alongside feminist groups. One said that 'there are a few women's lobbies that don't like men participating in feminism', suggesting they 'need a space on their own to feel safe' (Juan, Spain). More specifically, this meant that some women's groups did not like men participating in the annual march on 25 November for the Day for the Elimination of Violence Against Women. Since 1981, this date has been marked internationally in memory of the murder of the Mirabal sisters by the government of the Dominican Republic on 25 November 1960. One consequence was that profeminist men have organised their own marches and candlelit vigils against violence against women on 21 October every year, in a growing number of cities and towns, since the first one was held in Seville in 2006. These were open to men and women, and were organised intentionally to be separate from the November and March events to avoid encroaching on already existing women's events.

Similarly, in the UK there has been some criticism that the White Ribbon Campaign's primary day of action, 'White Ribbon Day', is held on 25 November because it could be seen as a symbolically important day of feminist activism being taken over by male anti-violence activists. However, at the same time, one of the Spanish interviewees described how early responses to such activities were deemed by many – men and women – to be a form of gender treachery: 'Back in the 1960s we always had sort of people bothering you, writing to you, telling you "you are a traitor" because women were taking the best part of it [already have the benefits in society]' (Jon, Spain).

It was certainly the case that some men felt that they were stuck between a rock and a hard place. Sometimes these views were expressed with an understanding about why women's organisations might be cautious or suspicious about men's involvement in anti-violence work, however on other occasions some of the interviewees appeared to feel that the violence against women field should be more receptive towards men. One interviewee discussed how, when he first started speaking out about violence against women, he would receive criticisms both from feminist and anti-feminist groups, highlighting the range of different viewpoints that have to be navigated when seeking to engage with men from a profeminist perspective:

> We would be challenged by both sides really, by the men's rights side saying we hate men, and from women's organisations obviously because of the risk of diverting funding which was definitely an accurate and legitimate worry to have, but also that we were apologists for men or overly optimistic for men. (James, UK)

We return to this issue of relationships with 'men's rights' groups later in the chapter. For now, we move on to look at a specific issue that can create conflict between men working in this area and women in the feminist violence against women movement.

'Male unicorns' – putting men on a pedestal

Frustratingly, it is a well-known phenomenon that men who become involved in speaking out publicly about their anti-violence against women work are often viewed and treated more positively than women who do the same work. They may be regarded as particularly 'unusual' – as special and indeed as rare and 'exotic' as a unicorn. In total, in our survey 65 per cent of men agreed or strongly agreed with the statement that 'men's voices and efforts receiving greater attention/ value than women's' is a possible risk of more men taking a public stance on violence against women.

This is what Messner, Greenberg and Peretz (2015) describe as the 'pedestal effect', which they define as 'a level of praise and escalating status men receive in feminist spaces that far outstrips what a man has actually accomplished or contributed' (138–139). As one of the interviewees in their study critically observed, 'I get up and say something that is anti-sexist, they think I'm Jesus Christ, Moses, and Santa Claus all wrapped up in one.' (Frank Blaney, in Messner, Greenberg and Peretz, 2015, 140).

In our research, there were certainly examples of this pedestal effect happening. However, there was variation in the levels of self-awareness and feelings of discomfort among the participants. In Sweden for example, two men described being treated like 'heroes' for the anti-violence work they did. For one of the interviewees, this made him feel uncomfortable – undermining some of his own profeminist 'messages' and also undermining the strength of women's own voices; for the other this was not such a problem.

The participant who found the pedestal effect uncomfortable described the strategies that he had developed in an attempt to diffuse it; choosing to exclusively mention the work and knowledge of women colleagues when asked about different aspects of his work, for example. Another strategy was to use the opportunity to put the focus back onto women's contributions in various work settings (eg at women's refuges/shelters) which had been operating and often struggling for a very long time.

> Some say 'it feels nice that you are coming, I've been standing here banging my head against the wall for five years now and not being able to get anywhere [with colleagues], so it feels good you're here.' And that sure is nice to hear, but it's also sad because the ones saying this are women who have often been working for a really long time with these issues, and then, along comes a man and everybody is like 'Aha!'. So, there are mixed feelings for my part, what I'm ascribed here. [...] So, if you approach a person who is going to give you money for a project; I can, as a man, place myself a little bit behind and like 'This is not us, we are just a support for the women's movement in this, and *she* is the one with all the competence.' Although it can still turn into 'How nice of you as a man to acknowledge this' and well [sighs with resignation]... (Dag, Sweden)

Another Swedish interviewee, Jack, expressed similar concerns. On the one hand, he accepted the praise and considered it a recognition and an appreciation. He was happy for the acknowledgement and confirmation he and his peer-group of men received when they participated in television and other media events discussing men's violence against women. On the other hand, he reflected on the situation as it was: 'Then in the 1990s, it was unusual that men became involved [in anti-violence activism], so it was a lot of media. Then you had these thoughts: have we now taken space in public life at the expense of women who have the done the same thing [as us] for years? We only have to say "we are feminists", then all cameras are there all of a sudden' (Jack, Sweden).

Perversely, it may be that this pedestal effect that in part undermines the very messages being put forward might also be a factor in getting more men engaged in this work. One interviewee highlighted that concern about being treated negatively rather than positively might be one of the barriers for men and boys getting involved. This negative treatment may come from peers or from any number of different directions:

> [They might think] if I did something about it, it might affect me negatively, as other men might see me as not someone they could do business with. If you get involved in it, then men will not react well if you start challenging them. Or talking about the systematic way in which men abuse women and are advantaged in relation to women. A lot of men won't react well. So it's almost as though the fact that other men aren't taking a public stance or are hostile – like 'I would get involved, it's just other men won't like it much'. I reckon a lot of men think like that. (Dean, UK)

Overtly stating some of the positives in terms of social status and positioning was therefore seen as one strategy for getting more men involved. One interviewee took this even further and reflected that maybe for those men (himself included?) that did not 'make it' in the 'bastion of male activity' might instead enjoy being centre stage in a community of women:

> The men would always go out on a Monday night for a drink, and once again I was treated as a bit of an oddity. They'd try to wind me up. But then I don't mind being different. And I think that's something about an ego thing. If I'm unusual, then I'm the centre of attention. And I think that, now I'm thinking about that, I do know some men

and maybe I'm one of them, who gets into this field because there's a paucity of men in this area and they're not very successful in the bastion of male activity. Oh god that's a not good thought! (Bob, UK)

James highlights the complex motivations at play:

> Going back to the knight in shining armour thing, there's an element of truth in you get praise for it, I don't want to overemphasise it, but there have been people who have said that must be difficult to do and well done. And that did make me feel good. Everyone's motivations are complex. (James, UK)

However, highlighting this as a potential positive in order to increase men's engagement would almost certainly have problems as an approach on multiple levels, including potentially constraining their relationships with feminist women and the women's movement, and the questionable motivations of men that might be attracted to becoming involved on this basis. There already exist serious and credible concerns that circulate on social media about the sexist and abusive behaviour of a small number of men who are held up as leaders in the global profeminist movement and critical masculinities field.

This awareness of a pedestal effect, combined with a difficulty navigating it, was the 'holding space' for most of the men who had engaged critically with anti-violence activism. By 'holding space', we mean that it is possible that this cannot and should not be seen as an obstacle that needs to be broken down, but rather that it is a tension that needs to be lived alongside, 'held' by continually asking questions of oneself such as those raised by Dean:

> Maybe there is an uncertainty among men about taking too much space, and displacing women's voices? Is it wanted, is it helpful? Maybe I'd be better off taking a step back as men are in the foreground too much? (Dean, UK)

The need for this continuous 'autoreflexivity' was also mentioned by Didac, one of the Spanish interviewees, in relation to the rewards of the pedestal effect.

'Talking the talk but not walking the walk'

Our survey also highlighted a range of other problematic issues which can sometimes arise when men become involved in efforts to end violence against women, and which are important to take into account. Approaching half – 48 per cent – of the men who responded agreed or strongly agreed with the statement that 'male activists not behaving in non-violent and gender equal ways' is a risk related to more men taking a public stance on violence against women.

Some were specifically concerned that men might get involved in anti-violence work without reflecting sufficiently on issues of masculinity and patriarchy, with one writing 'superficial change or support, not revising our own masculinity' (Sweden). Another felt there is a risk of 'dilution of the notion of violence against women and girls being gender biased' (UK). Similar to this, one commented that 'some of these men won't have an understanding of the impact of structural inequality, male privilege, misogyny and patriarchy and may espouse a "gender blind" approach, which may lead them to reinforce unhelpful messages' (UK).

Given there are (relatively) high profile cases of accusations being made of male allies using violence and abuse, it is surprising that just under half felt this was a risk. In Sweden for instance, there is an infamous case where a high-profile chief of police known as 'the Dress Captain' ('Kapten Klänning') working against gender discrimination, sexual harassment and men's violence against women within law enforcement sought out, raped and abused girls and young women and was convicted in court for these crimes in 2010. In our interviews, one interviewee talked about a case where a famous man in Australia who was seen as taking a profeminist stance was found to have been using violence and abuse himself. Subsequent to the data collection for this book, allegations have been made against high-profile academics and activists in the field internationally. In our interviews, men were concerned about how these actions would impact on other men being involved in this work:

> They do damage in all sorts of ways. They make women understandably very suspicious about men's involvement and commitment. And those men are abusive to women. They present themselves as being trustworthy, but they're not. That is part of the dominant discourse – men have a whole series of not very savoury reasons for getting involved in this stuff. (Dean, UK)

This raises questions about what men's groups can do to try to stop this happening and address it if and when it does happen. While there are no easy answers, the importance of accountability, having procedures in place to deal with it, encouraging self-reflection and honesty are all useful starting points.

The personal costs of being involved: being a 'gender traitor'

Some of the British interviewees discussed how men may feel reluctant to speak out about violence against women because it is perceived to go against the gendered status quo – that doing so may bring their masculine credentials into question, as it is seen as being something 'unmanly' to care about. Indeed, men may fear being viewed as a 'gender traitor' if they are too vocal about feminist issues and the oppression of women (Meadows, 2007). Even if they may agree in principle about ending violence against women then, fears about potentially emasculating themselves and facing consequences for this among other men and boys may present a barrier to openly expressing such beliefs. In this respect, one of the interviewees suggested that men's unwillingness to talk to one another about personal or sensitive issues such as violence and abuse presents another major obstacle, both in terms of encouraging them to challenge violence against women, and in talking about their own personal issues and difficulties, such as mental health problems.

This highlights the important role that can be played by organisations which are principally targeted at men and boys, to provide opportunities for them to speak out against violence towards women, discuss these issues with other men and boys and support one another in the process. It also shows the need for more men to play an active part in developing these organisations in support of the broader feminist movement to end violence against women.

The interviewees also experienced obstacles and struggles within their personal lives and with those around them (such as family members) in terms of their embrace of profeminism and anti-violence activism. This took several forms. One of the Swedish interviewees told us he has no contact with his family at all, though this is not only (or perhaps primarily) because of his anti-violence work. As mentioned earlier, another Swedish interviewee has encountered a more passive form of resistance from family members: since he moved to the city and many of his values and ideas changed (including about men and violence), his family has started to refer to him as 'the lost son'. In

Spain, some of the interviewees that were academics talked about the professional costs that working in this area had brought in their career paths – with them seen as studying 'secondary', 'women only matters'.

In Sweden, examples were more politicised while also being personal. Jack referred to earlier days: 'We received letters, with stamps. "Are you gays or sissys?" That was the net-hate [online abuse] of the time.' He remembered articles he wrote about men's responsibility at an early debate forum where he received a lot of comments, one of which labelled him as the feminists' 'pet dog'. 'It wasn't that threatening, but still, there is a hate.'

Kristian recounts the experience of always meeting some kind of resistance, often in small doses of objection in both personal conversations and organisational work.

> I have got this type of internet-hate and death threats a couple of times. For instance, when I wrote about the Sweden Democrats ('Sverigedemokraterna', the far-right party) and masculinity. Then the violent threats were instant, which makes you uneasy as hell. It is interesting to experience what that does to you, I mean the fear when someone describes a very 'grovt' (severe) violence that they are going to do to you. It is kind of scary. I haven't been so active in social media, so I have not gotten that much hate. But the times I've written… there is always resistance. Especially from men. Almost only from men. (Kristian, Sweden)

Other Swedish interviewees talked about receiving hate mail from other men. In Spain, hate mail was sent to profeminist men too, for example by calling them part of the 'feminazi' movement. Increasingly across all three countries, this 'hate mail' was moving online. Some efforts had been made in Spain to join together to develop a coordinated strategy against those sending hateful messages on social media, for example reporting them en masse to have them removed from the space.

One survey respondent also pointed out that there can be risks for men engaged in doing this work, too:

> I think there is also the personal cost – one which I gladly pay but which I think is often not discussed. To be a man who is active in challenging violence against women and girls, and who does that in a way that avoids asserting (consciously or not) male privilege, is to engage in a constant dialogue with self. That can bring about positive

benefits, but it also an on-going process, not least of listening, self-monitoring, etc. I think this needs to be considered more, if we are to teach men who take a public stance on violence against women, to develop and maintain this 'emotional' muscle. (UK)

This respondent illustrates the value that greater self-reflection can have for men and boys (and the people around them), and the transformative potential it can have for their lives. He also highlights that we rarely consider the costs that may be incurred by men (and indeed by women) who are involved in activism to end violence against women. This is understandable, given that the work is focused primarily on dismantling male privilege and supporting women in confronting the impacts of patriarchy on their lives. However, it is important to avoid replicating the idea that men are always 'tough' and 'invulnerable' within this work, by failing to consider the ways in which they may find it difficult and even traumatising at times, too. Some of our interviewees alluded to profeminist men having a tendency to feel like they have to take on a massive burden and try to 'solve' the problem all by themselves, often in quite a solitary way, for example. This again highlights the benefits of men involved in anti-violence and profeminist activism providing support for one another as much as possible, so they don't feel like they are going through the struggles involved in doing this work alone. It is these relationships with other men that we move to next.

Relationships with other men

Relationships with other men did not emerge as important in terms of *becoming* active or starting to work in the anti-violence movement, as discussed in Chapter 2. However, they *did* emerge as being important for some men in terms of maintaining their involvement in the work, often acting as a form of 'comradeship' which often moved into personal, lasting friendships. This was not the case for everyone though, and at least as many men talked more about having increasingly problematic friendships with men as supportive ones. Indeed, some of our participants had increasing difficulties in maintaining friendships with other men because they often revolved around macho or sexist behaviours that they felt uncomfortable about. There were also examples given of where men who were said to be allies to the end violence against women movement had acted in ways that were inconsistent with furthering the rights of women and ending men's violence.

We start by discussing the influence of men's relationships with other men at the micro level (in terms of personal, individual friendships) then move outwards to the macro, more political relationships, activities and interactions, including through men's groups, political demonstrations and also clashes with other men's groups loosely defined as the 'men's rights movement'.

Men as personal friends, peers and mentors

Many of the men talked about having problems with friendships with other men, largely because of the masculine expectations placed on them and the experience of being in large groups of men in particular. Even where men were involved in group activities such as football, men talked about not really sharing thoughts and feelings with each other. One participant told us how he had played football with the same group of men for 20 years yet barely knew anything about them (Iain, UK). This was even the case where men were involved in other social justice activist groups. As one recalled:

> I was with some activists who were working in another area. And they made a joke. 'Oh, I'd better not say anything, I'll get beaten up by my wife', and I was so incensed by their behaviour. Some of them stopped speaking to me. But I'm trying to be more ancillary now to get a better response, but still stick to the stance. And the one thing that still winds me up is 'what about the men'. And I'd be asked, 'can we make it gender neutral', and I'd say well it's not a gender-neutral subject! (Bob, UK)

This issue of being challenged by otherwise 'socially aware' male friends and family as to why men are specifically working on violence against *women* was also mentioned by another UK participant:

> He's [family member] liberal and socially aware, but he does think this narrative about gender violence and men's violence against women almost never mentions men's own experiences of violence. He would see it as 'unfair' and 'inaccurate' and part of the problem. So, it does alienate him, and makes him feel uncomfortable about things like the White Ribbon Campaign. He sees it as being, that it doesn't represent men's experience very well. (Dean, UK)

Within the field of violence against women specifically, some men found useful and supportive connections with other men who were doing similar work. While acknowledging that they had received more support from women than from men, there were some examples of individual supportive friendships. There were suggestions of differences between the three countries, whereby in Spain and Sweden there were male ally group-based friendships, while in the UK it tended to be more individual based, less organised and more variable in that some of the interviewees had connections with other male allies whereas others didn't. Friends, peers and/or mentors instead tended to be other men that they 'bumped into' and connected with at events that they happened to both be at. This is not to diminish this form of interaction, just to segment it from more sustained friendships where ongoing support existed outside of other events or in the form of informal groups where specific meetings or events were planned specifically to talk about being men in this area of work.

Some of our participants were optimistic that this was starting to change however, particularly in relation to a broader umbrella of 'masculinity issues' such as suicide, mental health and fatherhood becoming more widely discussed. It was also pointed out that some male celebrities were starting to initiate more conversations around these kinds of issues:

> I suppose there are also men in the public eye who are starting to articulate these things more, like Robert Webb. So, the landscape is changing, some of the social conditions are changing a bit. (Dean, UK)

Robert Webb is a UK comedian who wrote a popular book entitled *How Not to Be a Boy* (2017) about his experiences of growing up as a boy and a man, and the impact that expectations about masculinity have had on him and other people in his life. Similarly, a Spanish interviewee mentioned the influence of books by Octavio Salazar Benitez, a renowned Professor of Law, activist and author, such as *El Hombre que no Deberíamos Ser* (2018) which translates as 'The Man You Should Not Become – An Introductory Book About Feminism for Men'.

Men's groups

Semi-formalised men's groups were a route to supportive friendships for some of the interviewees. This was particularly mentioned by men in Spain as something that has been increasing. For example, one participant talked about how his men's group would provide both personal friendship as well as political planning:

> They [the men's group] would meet at the house of one of the men, and they would cook and do this 'men only' and deconstruct hegemonic masculinity and look at what they could do to create changes. (Didac, Spain)

In some other cases, one of the men in the group would reserve a private space in a restaurant and have dinner together and talk. These groups in Spain seem to have been increasing in number over the last three years.

In Sweden informal men's groups in the form of 'killmiddagar' or male-only 'supper clubs' under the label #guytalk or #killmiddag started as an initiative by the organisation MakeEqual in 2016, and has increased in Sweden post #MeToo with support from the organisation MÄN to do similar activities as in Spain and have similar discussions. These dinner sessions are often informal and focus on sensitive topics such as feelings, sexual harassment and violence with the help of conversational guides provided by gender equality organisations. A study by Olsson and Lauri (2020) addresses both the potential and the risks of using emotions and personal experience in such dinner meetings as a tool for political change. We did not hear of any examples like these in the UK happening in recent years, although two interviewees talked about being involved in such groups at university in the 1970s–80s.

> I helped organise a number of peer-led talks for men run by myself and other undergraduates at Oxford about various related issues. The title of the first talk was 'Are All Men Rapists?' and I was the presenter. I read some Andrea Dworkin, and Kate Millett and Juliet Mitchell. Really that and other talks were an opportunity for men to learn about the issues, explore what they thought, and work out what they might do about it. It was a discussion group. The first meeting had about 30 men, in about 1982. (Dean, UK)

Groups such as these existed in the 1970s in the UK in most towns and cities, although none of our UK participants talked about participating in this type of group in recent times. A number of support groups for men have been developed in the UK, such as 'men's sheds' and men's mental health groups, although it is unclear whether they have a political or activist stance alongside their health support and friendship mechanism. Meanwhile, organisations engaging with men and boys about gender equality in the UK, such as the Beyond Equality and the White Ribbon Campaign, do appear to hold internal activities and events for their volunteers to connect, share ideas and build a sense of community among one another.

Where they exist, men's groups of this kind that do provide friendship and talk about issues of gender and masculinity in various ways challenge the prevalent gender norm that men can't or don't connect with each other emotionally. Rather, there may be an opportunity here to open up more spaces of this nature. In Spain, the development of such groups has been seen as important enough in terms of engaging men in gender equality work that it has been supported by some public organisations.

Among the UK interviewees, while they stressed the importance of their friendships with feminist women, they talked far less about men in their lives supporting them. This highlights a potential difficulty – when there are already not very many men doing this work, it may lead to a sense of isolation. This may make sustaining anti-violence activism harder for some men, by providing few opportunities to discuss gender issues with other supportive, likeminded peers, which could enable them to develop their thinking and hold one another accountable.

Since completing the interviews and survey for this research, things have of course shifted with restrictions placed on travelling and meeting in person during the COVID-19 era. As a result, much of men's anti-violence work shifted into online forums. For example, MenEngage Europe worked to provide an online platform to increase support for members, so that they could share their experiences, ideas and challenges during the pandemic with one another, and counter an increased sense of isolation that some organisations and activists might be feeling.

Visible, political demonstrations with other men

When comparing the three countries that are part of this research, Spain stood out as having the most active and developed visible movement of men against violence towards women. This is not to say that they necessarily have the largest numbers of men, but that in terms of visible and overt political organising, they came the closest that we saw to a profeminist, anti-violence men's movement.

For instance, a few interviewees told us about several marches held in Seville, which when it was held in 2016 had between one and two thousand people in attendance, with a roughly even split of men and women. We were also told about regular vigils, demonstrations and marches involving men in Barcelona, Seville and Madrid.

At the same time, Pablo described how there had been a general problem in Spain for the last few years that social movements of different types had generally had difficulties mobilising, and that this had also been the case for the men's anti-violence movement. This led to some frustrations about the pace and scale of the work from some of the interviewees. However, they did acknowledge that even if the pace and scale were not as great as they would like, that they were still further ahead of many other countries.

> Comparing with other countries, I think Spain has a movement. We do make jokes, and say that it's not really 'a movement', but it is a small movement. In the media you can say Men for Equality, Hombres por la Igualdad, and they will know who you are referring to. There's perhaps 200, 300 people – men in every city or region in Spain who will be called periodically to appear in the media, to make statements and to support and all that. (Pablo, Spain)

Furthermore, since the interviews were conducted these political mobilisations have grown further, such as with the sparking of the #Cuéntalo and #YoSiTeCreo movements (the Spanish version of #MeToo) and the feminist strike in 2018, as discussed further in Chapter 4. In addition, the leaders of some Spanish social movements have recently entered into government, with the centre-left PSOE (Spanish Socialist Workers' Party) and radical left Unidas Podemos gaining power after the 2019 general election, and they have presented themselves as a 'feminist government'. As a result, some of the tensions in these movements have been playing out in the political sphere too, including disagreements between the two parties about how radical policies should be in relation to gender issues, such as making the legislation on rape and sexual violence more stringent.

As well as the political impacts of activities such as demonstrations and marches, the existence of a tangible movement of men working to end violence women, as can be seen in Spain, can also play an important role in providing support and enabling men to feel a sense that they are 'part of something'; that they are involved in a community of like-minded people rather than being isolated (Tolman et al, 2019).

These kinds of movement-building activities could therefore powerfully help to sustain men's involvement in anti-violence activism as well as recruiting more men to the cause.

Backlash politics – relationships with 'men's rights activists'

While there were positive examples of more men such as celebrities including comedians, authors and artists starting to speak out in the three countries, not only about gender-based violence but also broader issues relating to men (such as suicide, depression, restrictive gender norms and fatherhood), interviewees also highlighted challenges and tensions that can sometimes arise when men discuss and take action on these issues. This includes marginalising gender inequality as a whole and issues which primarily affect women, and hostility and backlashes towards women and feminism. In particular, concerns were raised in some of the interviews across the three countries about when an emphasis on issues affecting men and negative reactions to feminism are expressed by men in an organised way, including through the harmful influence of 'men's rights activists' (MRAs) in the UK. This has similarities to the Spanish concepts of 'neo-machismo' – an ideology to maintain male privileges in times of supposed equality between men and women (Lorente Acosta, 2009, 2018) or 'militant machismo'. In Sweden men's rights activism ('mansaktivister') is often focused on disputes over child contact, men subjected to violence from women and when men are accused of rape. More recently the activism is related to different strands of right-wing ideology and what Gottzén (2018, 2019) calls 'affective politics' (in other words, politics connected to emotions and feelings), located in the internet-based 'manosphere' with a focus on sexuality, such as alt-right misogynistic groups and incels ('involuntary celibates'). The men's rights movement has not been mobilised to the same extent as in the US and UK (Reeser and Gottzén, 2018). However, the far-right movement more broadly has gained political influence in the Swedish parliament in recent elections.

For instance, some of the Spanish participants described their concerns at how the hostility among some men towards feminism was being strengthened in the contemporary context by the emergence of vocal 'men's rights' groups, both there and elsewhere. As one interviewee put it:

> This movement has been there, but now is more active and aggressive. There's a backlash of men engaged in this movement of men's rights, and the agenda, which is based

on three things: custody of the children; saying that the law against gender violence has a lot of false demands; and the third one is that there is not real equality but discrimination against men... the uprising of these male 'machistos', as we call them, it's quite a problem. (Jon, Spain)

Another Spanish interviewee felt that men involved in the men's rights agenda are in some cases successfully using these ideas to get to a sector of the population, in particular the numerous unemployed and lower-paid working class, and encouraging them towards a reactionary anti-feminist, anti-immigration, nationalist – even fascist – discourse. Men's rights activism can thus be understood as a reaction to social, cultural and political developments in the field of gender equality, as well as other, broader changes in society (Greig, 2019). However, insights into the costs of masculinity for men may also work as an accelerator for engaging in anti-violence work, demonstrating the importance of anti-sexist men raising and addressing these issues from a profeminist perspective.

Men's rights groups were seen as a definite threat to men's anti-violence work and organising, and to efforts to end violence against women more broadly. Some of the survey respondents also pointed towards some additional risks that can arise in this regard. For example, two respondents highlighted dangers associated with an increased influence of anti-feminist men in society, with one writing: 'Co-option of male organisations doing good work to prevent VAWG by men seeking to use this agenda to promote more negative opinions' (UK). A Spanish respondent commented that 'The greatest risk is the reaction of the neo-machismo groups that are still very strong and have a lot of money thanks to the support of administrations and institutions such as the churches.' There is thus a danger that such groups can attract men who become interested in issues around gender, or feel some sense of grievance or dissatisfaction in relation to their position in society (perhaps connected to a sense of masculine entitlement), but who have not engaged with feminism or have reacted defensively and with hostility towards it (Flood, Dragiewicz and Pease, 2020). There is a real need for profeminist men's groups to provide a positive counterpoint to this and demonstrate to more men and boys the value of feminism and how it can help them to make sense of and deal with the problems they experience.

Summary

In Chapter 2 we described how women as individuals, as family members and within women's anti-violence organisations were important in supporting men to become involved and to start speaking out publicly about violence against women. This chapter has shown that their role in supporting men once they were involved in this area of activism is also an important one. Where men were challenged by women about their involvement, this critique was both given and received in different ways. Likewise, both the challenges and the opportunities involved in the 'pedestal effect' were also experienced and acted upon in different ways. There was not a clear division in terms of how this was experienced by men from different counties.

Just as there were different (though generally positive) experiences of interactions with the women's movement, so too were there different experiences of interactions with other men. Whereas men as individuals or within groups or organisations did not play a significant role in supporting men to engage, they did emerge as more important for men once they were involved. Some of this was at a level of support, providing 'comradeship' either as an individual friendship or as part of a group. Such group support was less likely in the UK compared to Sweden or Spain. On a political, activist level, the UK lagged behind in terms of men organising to end violence against women together, with Spain holding public actions on a scale that the UK feels a long way away from achieving. With greater notoriety and support though came a greater visible backlash, and men in Sweden and Spain talked more in their interviews than men in the UK sample about negative experiences with men who were hostile to the violence against women movement (so called 'men's rights activists').

Certainly, there was a situation where some men were stuck between a rock and a hard place – they were not part of the feminist women's movement, but were not (at least for most of the men we interviewed) fully part of a dynamic, progressive men's movement. Some men were positioned as an 'outsider' to some extent from other men; some interviewees found it difficult to join in with traditional male friendship groups. Others did have these groups, for example through sports teams, but received little to no personal support through these friendship groups in relation to their work on violence against women. Meanwhile, while the potential threats of men to the women's movement were acknowledged to some extent, the new threat on the horizon is undoubtably an ideological backlash from other men's groups in the form of 'men's rights activists' and potentially wider society generally.

4

Getting more men involved

In his book on anti-sexist men, Christian wrote in 1994 that the men whose life stories are presented in his book are probably an 'untypical minority' (1994: 4), but that he hoped it would be a road that more men will travel down in the future. Unfortunately, it remains the case today that the stories that are contained within our book still represent a somewhat 'untypical minority'. Indeed, one of the primary purposes of this book is to see how this may become a more common route for more men in the future, and it is this topic that we turn our attention to in this chapter. Using the interviews and survey results, we look at the contexts that our participants felt were more and less conducive to men speaking out publicly about men's violence against women, before considering some of the positives that we might build on in this regard, and then some of the obstacles. Some of these obstacles are ones that might need to be overcome, while others are likely to be more fixed and need men to be able to navigate or sit alongside rather than to actively try to overcome them.

Who is involved? Which men speak out?

In Chapter 2 we explored the individual motivations for the men in our interview sample to become involved. Here we are more concerned about the social, cultural, political and economic issues that might make it easier or more likely that men within particular social groups or contexts will think critically about violence against women and consider taking profeminist action. Developing our knowledge about the influence that these factors can have is useful, not least because it may help us learn how we can stimulate more conducive conditions for men to speak out. In both the survey and the interviews, we asked whether participants had found there to be any particular groups of men they thought might be more likely to take action. The survey asked respondents to state to what extent they agreed with a series of statements and make brief follow up comments, whereas the interview allowed this to be explored in greater depth. There was greatest agreement that men who were already involved in other social movements (eg anti-racist, vegetarianism/animal rights and environmental movements) were more likely to also take a public stance on violence against women – with 97 per cent of the survey respondents agreeing with this. One UK survey respondent added that 'In my own experience, politically active young men who are part of other equality movements are most likely to take a public stance against VAWG [Violence against women and girls].'

By contrast, no respondents felt that men in either right-wing political groups or men with power (eg in politics, business, media, law) were more likely to take a public stance. This was also echoed within some of the interviews, where some of the respondents worked to influence these fields (and men in them):

> From experience I'd say libertarian and right-wing individuals are least likely to appreciate or talk about such issues, particularly those who are wealthy. Those with entrenched privileges often protect many more than the privileges they directly benefit from. (Luke, UK)

Indeed, one of the survey respondents pointed out that there can be particular risks when such men are involved:

> I think there does also need to be a conversation about men who take an active stance in public against violence against women but in their private lives do not live according to this. These men are present in the movement, and are perhaps more likely to be stepping into this world (say because they are signed up as senior leaders in politics, government, business). They are recruited because they bring 'heft' but sometimes that feels like it gives them a pass that means their wider commitment is not questioned. (UK)

Therefore, there may be particular cautions applied to the motivations of senior leaders who gain a lot of publicity in this area at key points in their careers, for example around election times.

Many of the respondents also felt that sexuality and gender identity were potentially influential factors, with 65 per cent agreeing that gay or bisexual men and 60 per cent agreeing that trans men were likely to speak out. Meanwhile, several respondents (38 per cent) believed that young men were more likely to take a public stance, with one writing that 'young people concerned by social problems I think are more likely to also be interested in preventing gender violence' (Spain). Many interviewees also pointed to the importance of encouraging more boys and young men to become involved, which we return to later in this chapter.

There was a mixture of views about the influence of privilege in encouraging men to take action against violence towards women; 30 per cent of respondents felt that middle-class men were more likely to speak out, for example, with one stating that 'middle-class men may make up more of this group as their wealth could buy them the time to do so' (UK). However, 19 per cent agreed that disabled men, and 14 per cent agreed that men from ethnic minorities, might be more likely than other men to take a public stance, with one Swedish respondent commenting that 'I think any individual with experience from discrimination are more likely to take a stance against other forms of discrimination'. Another noted that men who are themselves marginalised in different ways, such as men from ethnic minority backgrounds or gay or trans men, might be no less likely to sympathise with ending violence against women, but might be preoccupied with their own struggles, as they 'have other causes that they fight for and risk more by taking public stances' (Spain). On the other hand, they may already be experienced at speaking out about another cause, and this experience could be extended to activism to end violence against women. Some of the participants also added that men who had themselves experienced some form of violence might be more inclined to speak out. This was also mentioned by Luke in the UK interviews, although he highlights that this is far from inevitable:

> Instinctively, you'd think men who have suffered at the hands of other men are probably the most likely to speak out. However, this is not always the case as it's also common for men to perpetuate precisely the norms they have encountered in the past, no matter how much they've been harmed by them. In fact, some men who've suffered intensely at the hands of other men can be the most vocal supporters of masculine norms. (Luke, UK)

Despite the list of options that we offered in the survey, some felt that these factors were not particularly important, with one commenting: 'I'm not sure that any of these groups are more likely to take a public stance, to be honest; I think it depends on their life experiences and, particularly, their exposure to feminist thought' (UK). This perspective was also reflected in the interviewees' different experiences outlined in Chapter 2 of how they came to be involved, despite having a range of different backgrounds and social circumstances.

Where are men involved? Where do men take a public stance?

Nearly all of our respondents (87 per cent) felt that men were particularly likely to take a public stance against violence against women in the context of non-governmental, voluntary or community organisations. This also reflected the sample of men who participated in our research in both the interviews and the survey, who were mainly from NGOs and worked in either a paid or a voluntary capacity (as described in Chapter 1).

One suggested that this was because men 'are more likely to be exposed to feminist arguments' (UK) in such settings. This was also mentioned within the interviews, with one interviewee comparing it with other workplaces:

> Maybe as a man working in the voluntary or community sector you would be exposed to more feminist ideas. This is probably stronger in certain contexts... there are plenty of organisations where you won't be exposed to those ideas. For example in the city, or in an engineering firm, or on a building site. (Dean, UK)

Many (68 per cent) also felt that men in socialist or left-wing political groups were more likely to speak out, although one Swedish respondent noted that 'there are a lot of men in socialist groups who consider it a "diversion" or luxury to be handled after capitalism has fallen'.

Meanwhile, large numbers of respondents selected working in social services (58 per cent), schools, colleges or universities (55 per cent) and healthcare services (53 per cent) as being contexts in which men were also more likely to speak out. One tied this to 'settings in which empathy and caring for others are valued' (Spain). Another wrote as follows:

> I think any educational setting where ideas and ideology are challenged are likely to be more fertile ground, particularly schools, as toxic sexist beliefs and attitudes are less likely to be entrenched. Social Services and local government are more likely to have anti discriminatory policies and procedures and equality training. I'd say the same is true for many NGO's, but this is probably more variable. (UK)

Higher education was also mentioned in this respect by some of the interview participants, because it is a space in which students and staff alike have many opportunities to openly learn about and discuss feminism and issues of men's violence against women as part of day-to-day life within the institution. For example, one of the interviewees talked about how working in a university enabled him to educate hundreds of students each year about different forms of gender-based violence:

> One of the benefits is that not only do I have this research interest and can teach my students, it's that I'm in an HE [Higher Education] setting, so I can discuss this with my students, and this has a benefit not only on them but also on other people in their lives. So one of my students was reading my book, and she went to work and left it on the table, and her mum sat down and read it! And she said I didn't know that these were the issues, and I thought how lucky am I, not only had an impact on my student but also the family members who are not on the course! … So I'm really grateful and for a man in my position it's really helped me to take a public stance. I don't think I'd have had that avenue to release my views and opinions if I wasn't within the HE sector. (Abbas, UK)

Furthermore, universities are filled with young people who some of the participants felt would be less likely to hold sexist attitudes, and more willing to think openly and critically about gender relations. That is not to say that men's violence against women is not also enacted within these environments – far from it. However, some of the interviewees felt that they might be more conducive settings for men to take action against it. Meanwhile, one participant described how shifting attitudes among young people was a source of hope for him:

> I heard about some Fawcett Society [UK feminist NGO] research which surveyed younger and older men and showed that older men tend to have less positive attitudes to gender equality. You ask men whether they are positively disposed to gender equality, and a higher proportion of younger men are. I find that optimistic. (Dean, UK)

Overall, smaller amounts of respondents in the survey felt that men might be more likely to take a public stance in the police and crime agencies (16 per cent) and in local government (13 per cent).

Regarding the police context, one Swedish respondent remarked that 'I think police are very hard on the particularly savage violence against women, but don't take more common forms of harassment and abuse very seriously'. Some of the participants in both the survey and in the interviews also mentioned sports clubs and institutions as being an additional context in which men might be more likely to take action, maybe because this is a place where men are present in large numbers. At the same time, sport was also used in some interviews as an example of environments where problematic norms of masculinity are present and cultivated.

While these responses suggest that some organisational contexts might be more conducive for men to speak out about violence against women than others, some of the survey respondents also emphasised that efforts should be made to engage with men in all settings: 'It's worth trying to attract men wherever they are, especially if it's about places of men in transformation (social services, schools, sport organisations...)' (Spain). We now turn to the theme of how to get more men involved, wherever they are located.

How to get more men involved

There was very little disagreement with any of the issues we suggested in the survey as possible factors which may help to encourage men to speak out. The factors which appeared to be most important for respondents were: knowledge of the issues around men's violence against women (55 per cent strongly agreed, 45 per cent agreed), female family member or friend experiencing men's violence (58 per cent strongly agreed, 40 per cent agreed), knowledge of feminist perspectives (55 per cent strongly agreed, 40 per cent agreed), training on preventing violence against women as part of job or role (48 per cent strongly agreed, 45 per cent agreed), and contact with profeminist men (60 per cent strongly agreed, 30 per cent agreed). However, the high levels of agreement with all options for this question suggests that participants generally felt that each of these factors could potentially play an important positive role in helping to encourage men to take a public stance against violence towards women, rather than there being some factors which are significantly more important than others. For instance, one respondent wrote:

> I think that it depends much from person to person what is effective and what and whether how much a certain intervention has an effect. I think that has happened in the

#MeToo campaign in Sweden, a combination of friends and family and the massive wave of women, in general, have had a fantastic effect on many men that earlier hadn't been acting. (Sweden)

We will return to the #MeToo campaign later in this chapter. The respondents also suggested some additional factors which could potentially play an encouraging role too, including: 'seeing male leaders (famous actors, politicians or other men that are admired) be openly

Figure 3: Factors most likely to encourage men to take a public stance on violence against women, n = 40

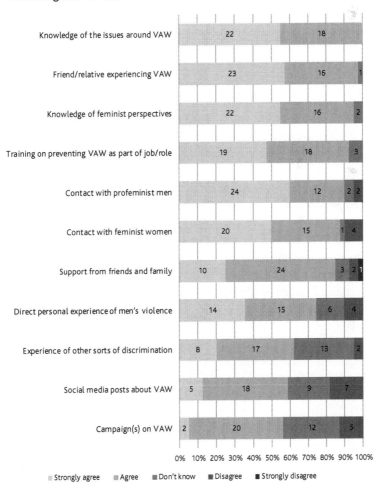

feminist and against VAW' (Spain), having 'religious convictions' (UK) and possessing 'self-awareness and an openness to criticism' (UK).

Education as the key

Probably the most constant theme throughout both the interviews and the survey from all countries was the need for the education of children and young people to change in a substantial way. Education and level of knowledge was returned to on a number of occasions as a strong thread that connected many of the other themes. In the survey, the suggested changes which received the highest levels of backing in relation to priorities for future change were: education on gender equality in school for all children (80 per cent strongly agreed, 20 per cent agreed); more education and awareness programmes targeting young men (75 per cent strongly agreed, 25 per cent agreed) and more training in workplaces and communities on preventing violence against women (63 per cent strongly agreed, 35 per cent agreed).

In the interviews, there were some overlaps with calls for educational programmes in schools around respectful relationships and consent, or in other words about the role of education in ending violence against women and girls generally. However, this is also specific to engaging more men and boys in the conversation as well. Calls for greater education also went beyond 'relationships and sex education' type courses to a broader equalities education. Many participants highlighted the need for a broad citizenship education which covered all age groups:

> Education. We need to educate men. Because I don't think men understand that this is a particular problem. If I had a magical wand then I would say that we need to educate men and women about their rights and responsibilities. (Abbas, UK)

The mentioning of a 'magical wand' can be interpreted as education being the foremost remedy for tackling men's violence. Education about equality was highlighted as being important over the life course in both the interviews and the surveys – in pre-schools as well as schools:

> We need to educate in equality, from nursery school onwards, real equality. (Didac, Spain)

> If we want to make an impact on more boys, I think we would need a progressive approach in pre-schools and the

early years of school to truly have a gender transformative setting [...] Let's say that we would have as an integrated part of our system that men could go and talk to other men, with leaders who have a clear gender transformative understanding. And then you would have gender transformative pre-schools. That could both impact on grown-ups at the same time as on children. So, that was something that I think is so important. (Patrik, Sweden)

Hence, it is important to consider integration with both curricula and the educational settings in which to make the most holistic approach. However, this holistic approach needs to be specific to the community and culture within which the school is based:

I think it all depends on the context that they've been brought up in, it doesn't matter what ethnicity, class, disability, whatever, if you're brought up to know something is wrong. Each community, each culture, each religion, you've got people in those communities who experience violence no matter what the culture is [...] If men are not educated in this area they are less likely [to take] a public stance, if they are more knowledgeable then they will. (Abbas, UK)

As part of this, there was a recognition that this type of education, as with relationships and sex education in some schools, was influenced by politics, with right wing governments arguing against or even removing such topics from curricula (this has especially been the case in Spain and until recently in the UK). Alongside the lack of specific equality-based citizenship education was discussion about the general invisibility of women across the curriculum. In history lessons, for example, instances were given of only teaching topics from a men's perspective which could lead to students assuming that the vote was given to women at the same time as men or not considering the role of women within major world events.

Going beyond the violence against women and girls sphere, and understanding more fully the role that inequalities in schooling have in terms of gender and other intersecting relations of power, was therefore seen as linked to much wider issues. Gender segregated schools, particularly religious or fee paying, were discussed in some of the Spanish and the UK interviews with a view that such segregation should no longer be allowed – segregation that has long been banned in Sweden. In addition, the gendered nature of the educational sector in terms of the higher ratio of women to men working as teachers, as nursery and pre-school staff and as providing care more generally was criticised. It was suggested that there should be higher value and pay for these sectors, and that his may also encourage more men to become involved. This would result in a workforce that better represented the communities they were working in.

This is not to say that there were not examples of where this kind of teaching was happening in educational settings, rather that these examples were piecemeal instead of being integrated across curricula. They were often delivered as one off 'projects', projects our interviewees were sometimes involved in, for example providing workshops in schools about non-sexist language, masculinity or gender-based violence.

Just as higher education in particular emerged as one of the 'routes in' for some of the men who participated in this research (discussed in Chapter 2), it follows that many participants saw higher education as an ideal place to engage more men. In other words, because they themselves had become switched on to the issues while at university, it followed that others would also be:

> We've been trying to do a lot of work with undergraduates when they arrive on the campus, trying to think about how do we try and set some cultural norms about how we expect people to behave, and really trying to work really hard at not preaching at students, but actually getting students to be seen to be taking the lead, and setting the tone. So, for example, we're doing a lot of work with our clubs and societies and asking our clubs and societies to help set the culture, that we want there to be across the rest of the university. [...] So I think there are opportunities where, it's trying not to say to men, you're the problem, but trying to reframe it to say, actually there is a problem here, it is a gendered problem, but actually we as men have a responsibility to be part of the solution. (Christopher, UK)

Education therefore was presented largely as an opportunity to get more men involved in the future, while the lack of such knowledge and awareness was seen as a barrier to getting men involved later on in life. The lack of education in wider society about issues of gender inequality can mean that a lot of work is required before men can arrive at a point at which they may feel able to speak out in an informed and confident way about violence against women. This also requires a degree of prioritisation and commitment to the issue by men themselves, which was an additional barrier pointed to by interviewees. Several participants discussed how many men may simply not think carefully about violence against women in the first place, and certainly not as something which has relevance to their lives, for instance because it is often perceived or framed as being a 'women's issue'.

Indeed, some of the participants felt their own ignorance as a man in relation to violence against women and other feminist issues had prevented them from giving these topics serious thought and attention for large parts of their lives. One interviewee cited the example of being asked to give talks and workshops in prisons for male perpetrators of violence. For him, this was an activity that was a responsibility for men to take on – for men to have the knowledge and awareness to pass on to other men. Another participant also highlighted that it is important that men are visibly leading some of this training:

> For us to be constantly having, say, men like you and I, standing up and talking about these issues. Not that it's about you and I talking about it, but that it's seen as, men and women are talking about it, and referring it back to practice, and what does it look like in practice. Yeah so I think that there is definitely scope for both workplaces and other places where men can be, and should be, seen very visibly, as taking some of the lead on these issues. (Christopher, UK)

It was noted that one of the ways in which male privilege functions is to blind men from many of the injustices within patriarchy, and that an unwillingness to confront this privilege can then provide a further obstacle to men taking action.

Swedish interviewees also pointed to the need to educate men, for instance in workplaces, on issues of gender and violence. Despite the fact that men tend to believe their levels of knowledge on gender equality in Sweden in relation to work and family are relatively high, issues of violence are not always 'on the table' to the same extent within these claims. Here, Patrik reflects on reaching both men and women in educational settings:

> The kind of image now that we are gender equal [is not helpful]. So, when you then work with a specific goal of stopping men's violence against women, it is easy for people to dismiss it by 'blaming' only certain men, special men [...]

so I think that has been something that I have met that they can sit there and listen, there is very little resistance. But when you come to talk a little bit more about it, then you see that many are satisfied with the notion that 'Yeah, of course it's terrible when there are some men raping and some men using violence, but there must be some and they must be a little bit special'. So, for me this a real obstacle today, to try to reach groups of men and some women. It's much easier I think to reach the women. They live with this. (Patrik, Sweden)

The media were seen by many as being playing a key role in passing on knowledge about violence against women. Most of the survey respondents agreed that positive media messages about what men and boys can do was important (63 per cent strongly agreed, 37 per cent agreed). Social media was also highlighted as important. In Spain, for example, interviewees talked about the important role that both traditional and social media had played over recent years in spreading knowledge about the extent and consequences of violence against women. This was seen as helpful in starting to build a critical mass which would be more favourable to more men speaking out about violence against women.

It can be relatively simple and comforting to believe in an optimistic and hopeful message of education reducing and eventually ending men's violence against women. But it is also something that is very difficult to evidence the impact of, over the short term at least. This ambiguity about social education was hinted at occasionally by some of the interviewees. For example, an UK interviewee (Iain) highlighted that highly educated men in privileged positions also commit violence and abuse. As more and more male students engage in mandatory or voluntary sessions on sexual consent and respectful relationships at university, if education is indeed as important as it is thought to be, we should start to see levels of violence drop among university educated men. This seems optimistic however, if the structures of gender inequality more broadly remain in place. Therefore, there should also be caution alongside calls for more education, with this being seen as one of the crucial pillars for change rather than the sole response needed.

Encouraging men involved in other social justice related struggles

Some of the men in both the interviews and the survey felt it was difficult or impossible to identify a particular 'group' or 'type' of man who might be more likely than others to become involved in anti-violence activism. The nearest they could get to this was men involved in social justice related struggles. In other words, men who have themselves experienced forms of prejudice, discrimination or marginalisation such as racism or homophobia, or are campaigning on these issues, may in turn be more likely to be able to recognise, empathise with and understand the oppression of women. As one of the Spanish interviewees put it, 'they are in some way already pro-equality' (Jon, Spain) even if not anti-violence.

This speaking out by 'pro-equality men' about other masculinity issues alongside men's violence, such as the rate of male suicide and men having poor relationships with other men, was also seen as important in terms of opening up conversations and changing social conditions. As one of the UK interviewees explained:

> There is a group of emerging men who care a lot about these issues. I would say they care, not necessarily equally, but certainly strongly about gender violence and about other gender-related issues, such as the rate of men's suicide, men having poor relationships with other men, a range of gender issues. And they care about them all. And if you ask yourself, what are they doing about it, if you look at an organisation like 'Great Men' (UK-based gender equality organisation working with men and boys, which subsequently merged with the Good Lad Initiative), there is a group of activists – of men who on a voluntary basis are doing something about it. What are they doing? They're talking to younger men about it, so they're not manning the barricades, they're doing something public, but on a more micro level. And I think that's significant. A space that men are starting to inhabit. Conversations with other men about the issues. I think what we haven't really got very much of is men and women talking to each other and working together. I think it is still quite separate to what female activists are doing. (Dean, UK)

Men who have faced prejudice because of their sexuality or their gender identity were also mentioned as those who might be more likely to speak out:

> I would say there is a disproportionate number of gay men involved, perhaps because they have a higher likelihood of experiencing violence and abuse themselves compared to

heterosexual men, so that might create a greater desire to provide emotional support to others. (Matthew, UK)

Gay men would have reasons to engage around gender and sexuality, and a lot of them have, much more than any other groups of men, very publicly. I don't mean around gender violence, but around gender issues. (Dean, UK)

Dean then went on to add:

I think men who are non-cis – in some way they don't fit the stereotype of hegemonic masculinity. (Dean, UK)

On the other hand, men without experience of other inequalities may be less likely to have this insight or experience:

People have a hard time understanding things that they do not themselves experience first-hand […] it's really difficult if those men are, you know, white, middle class. It's really difficult because they have to have something, I mean, in my case it was because of this something that I could make this imaginary leap. (Amel, Sweden)

Being alert to class-based inequalities was also mentioned, with trade unionists given as a particular example of a group of men who it might be possible to encourage to become active in tackling men's violence against women:

We are living in a time that is largely de-unionised in Britain. And whilst the labour movement has always carried with it manifestations of patriarchy, it has also carried with it notions of common struggle and solidarity, which present fantastic learning opportunities for men as fellow strugglers with women. (Robert, UK)

Robert then expanded on this point further:

Becoming more genuinely economically aware should provide a springboard for further action. For example, knowing about the disproportionate impact that austerity has on women. So rather than a particular economic position necessarily, an understanding of how economics and inequality affects people. (Robert, UK)

Islamophobia was also mentioned as an area of discrimination that could bring insights into other forms of inequality, and as a result meant that Islamic activities potentially provided a valuable setting for speaking out about sexism and violence against women. One of our participants highlighted the huge numbers of men coming together for religious celebrations such as Eid and the (generally missed) opportunities for engaging with men and boys about gender equality issues.

> Those organisations need to take a new response, including giving women equal voices, equal space, having more women on boards and also to talk about these issues to congregations. For example during Eid – Birmingham central mosque has around 4,000 per prayer, these are the perfect opportunities to talk about issues like violence against women, also in Friday prayers when it's obligatory for men to attend. There are thousands of men there. But my experience is that mosques don't want to talk about this. Perhaps they don't want to admit there is a problem, they want to maintain the status quo, they don't want to raise issues relating to Islam and increase Islamophobia, and because they simply don't know how to respond to it. And I would say that because I'm Muslim myself, but it could also be relevant to churches, temples, synagogues. The same can also be said of other religious institutions. (Abbas, UK)

Hence, there is a need for further research to understand the potential of engaging with men in different religious communities on the topic of violence against women.

Amplifying the voices and activism of working-class men and boys

In their interviews, some men spoke about the opportunity to engage more working-class men, noting that although the men involved in anti-violence activism were diverse in many other ways, they did tend to be middle-class with a high level of formal education. Social class was therefore sometimes mentioned as an opportunity to get more men involved, even if there may be additional barriers. One Spanish interviewee argued that working-class men were most difficult to engage on the issue of tackling violence against women, because many felt they had themselves been left behind and forgotten:

> Men from the working-class who have lost their jobs and their welfare coverage, their benefits; these are a very difficult sector. They are suffering a lot from the crisis of masculinity, if you can call it such. (Didac, Spain)

This interviewee said he and others had been working with some of these men in poor neighbourhoods in a southern Spanish city, and the difficulties there were real:

> You see men without identity and clinging to stereotypes and the past, and coming to confront the reality that they are not any more the breadwinners (Didac, Spain)

Having said this, he felt that some working-class men understand the women's rights movement and are not wholly resistant to change. He suggested the middle classes have more of a formal attitude to equality, 'but it is a way of resistance. It's saying 'well, I'm for equality of course, equality's already there'; 'a man and a woman have nowadays the same opportunities'. However, this attitude can be used to mask the reality of continuing inequalities, which we pick up again later in the chapter as a notable obstacle.

Generational differences

Several of the Swedish interviewees felt that there might well be generational differences in Sweden in which younger men are more willing to question the gendered status quo. One respondent suggested that involvement in organisations challenging men's violence might offer a valuable pathway into civil society for young ethnic minority men from the suburbs ('förorter') who are otherwise often excluded from mainstream society:

> It's a way to enter society, to understand 'Ah shit, there is another world, which is open to me'. Where the labour market is closed, politics may be closed, but civil society is a place which is really democratic, I would say, or most of the time. (Lucas, Sweden)

Another Spanish interviewee described how men in contemporary Spain often distance themselves from the behaviour of their parents or grandparents, stating: 'my grandfather was a "machist" [chauvinist] man, beat my grandmother. I don't do that' (Jon, Spain). He reflected that much of the Spanish middle-class felt themselves to be 'post-machist' [post-chauvinistic]. His organisation was often asked to give talks about 'new masculinities, meaning that there are new ways of being men who are not so traditional'. Although he felt that this was true, in many cases he thought inequalities were reproduced in other ways. For instance, Jon highlighted that many men felt gender equality had been attained, or even had gone too far.

There were some differences among Spanish interviewees in the extent to which they felt age might affect whether men were likely to take action against violence against women. Interviewees gave examples of organisations working with men from a profeminist perspective where there were more older men, with one commenting that:

> There is a sort of ageing of the people who have been engaged in this movement. We are quite old now and you don't see young people coming with their own voice as men against violence. (Jon, Spain)

On the other hand, other Spanish participants pointed to a potential new surge of younger men becoming involved, particularly in the larger cities such as Seville, Madrid, Valencia and in the Basque Country (mainly following the 8 March 2018 mobilisations, the #MeToo movement and the 'La Manada' trial). Alberto felt strongly that things were changing, given the numbers of men who were becoming involved:

> In the last few years, I believe that there is a clear advance in young non-organised male activism – both in terms of public issues against violence against women and also in their individual behaviours [...] Men's behaviours are changing. (Alberto, Spain)

One Swedish participant also suggested that given the diverging experiences and perspectives among different age groups, encouraging inter-generational discussions could be a productive and educational way of engaging with men and boys:

> It would facilitate for the learning to go both ways over generations. If you have a grandfather who could actually

talk to his grandchildren about stuff that he would have loved to not need to live with as a kid, if you have that dialogue you open up a lot. And grandmothers. And to... also to collectivise that discussion, so it's not only two-person, intimate relationship, but to stimulate it to be... you know, open it up, that discussion. (Noah, Sweden)

Although it was argued that young men were less traditional in their attitudes, and increasingly keen to take part in politics generally, this was 'not anymore through a specific movement of men'. One of the Swedish interviewees, with lengthy experience of activism against men's violence, suggested that this field had gone through several stages in Sweden. He now saw the current trend as moving away from a collective approach, to a view that such work starts with individual self-reflection. This trend may also be occurring elsewhere including in the UK, as social movements and identity politics have shifted over recent years, and while self-reflection is vital, it may also suggest that an individualised approach has increasingly become influential.

What obstacles are there to men taking action?

Next, we move onto looking at some of the obstacles we face in encouraging more men to get involved in the future. Looking at the survey first, respondents were asked about which factors they felt were most likely to prevent men from taking a public stance about men's violence against women.

In contrast to factors that could work to encourage participation, the factors that respondents thought could provide the biggest obstacles to men speaking out were: having a lack of interest or motivation (46 per cent strongly agreed, 54 per cent agreed); an indifference or hostility to women's rights (67 per cent strongly agreed, 28 per cent agreed); seeing violence against women as a 'women's issue' alone (41 per cent strongly agreed, 49 per cent agreed); having a lack of confidence to take action (23 per cent strongly agreed, 62 per cent agreed) or having a lack of training on preventing violence against women (21 per cent strongly agreed, 64 per cent agreed). The survey responses indicate that many different factors can potentially provide barriers to men speaking out about men's violence against women – however, the fact that several respondents did disagree with some of these factors suggests that they are unlikely to be insurmountable challenges. One survey respondent pointed out that the factors he disagreed with 'sometimes are used as

Figure 4: Factors most likely to prevent men from taking a public stance on violence against women, n = 39

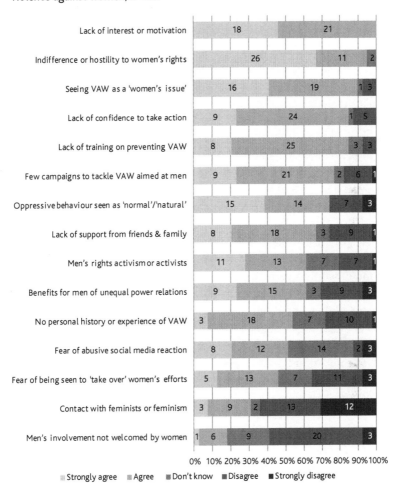

excuses for not getting involved' (Sweden) rather than being genuine reasons for a lack of action from men.

The survey respondents also suggested a few additional factors to take into account as possible obstacles to men taking a public stance against violence towards women: 'men are raised to first of all focus on [their] own issues and priorities, second focus on belonging to the male group' (Sweden), the 'thought of women's rights as already accomplished' (Spain), and 'defensiveness (eg seeing criticism of male violence against women as criticism of all men, in other words "not all men" syndrome) Guilt, which I would say is the biggest factor!' (UK).

While the majority of respondents agreed with most of the factors we suggested as being potential obstacles, this was not the case for all of the suggested factors. Most disagreed (51 per cent) or strongly disagreed (8 per cent) that men's involvement would not be welcomed by women's groups, with only 15 per cent agreeing and 3 per cent strongly agreeing (23 per cent were not sure). A majority also disagreed (33 per cent) or strongly disagreed (31 per cent) that contact with feminists or feminism would deter men from speaking out, although 23 per cent did agree and 8 per cent strongly agreed that this could discourage men. Some men disagreed (28 per cent) or strongly disagreed (8 per cent) that men would be put off by a fear of being seen as 'taking over' women's campaigns, although 33 per cent did agree and 13 per cent strongly agreed that this could be a factor. These responses were notable, as they suggest that most of the respondents had positive interactions with feminist women in their work, which conflicts with the assumption that men's work to end violence against women will not be welcomed by feminists. Meanwhile, a relatively large number of participants (36 per cent) didn't know whether men might be put off by a fear of an abusive social media reaction (while 21 per cent strongly agreed, 31 per cent agreed, 5 per cent disagreed and 8 per cent strongly disagreed), perhaps indicating that it can be hard to predict how different people will respond to reactions they receive, or the fear that such reactions will occur.

Strong gender equality discourse

Although it might be assumed to be an opportunity, in Sweden many of the respondents identified the country's strong gender equality discourse as presenting an obstacle. There were various nuances within this argument across the different interviews. For instance, one man suggested that in certain respects there are considerable limits on how far this discourse is translated into practice, and that those limits are even greater in relation to some gendered issues. For example, relatively few men are willing to look closely at the levels of violence towards women in Sweden, and perhaps even fewer are willing to explore the actual sexual practices of men and the myriad objectifications of women in Swedish society.

> Yes, the [idea of Swedish gender equality] can be a 'spoke in the wheel' sometimes. Because 'we are gender equal,

right?' And then when we start to look closer at it, people get disappointed, that 'oh, it wasn't that gender equal'. If we add on to that aspect; men trying to be active parents, we worked on that in this gender equality context [...], by equal paid parental leave and to stay at home just as much. Then comes the violence. And on that, there are not so many men engaged. And I believe that there is another aspect here concerning issues of prostitution, on men's sexual practices, some kind of core in patriarchal thinking. Over there [in that work on patriarchal thinking] there are hardly any men at all, digging deep into issues of men's sexual practices and the objectification of women and others. Over there, it's like, only shelter movement women ('jourkvinnor') and girls there, pushing this issue. (Dag, Sweden)

This can be linked to a focus on creating 'good men' within Swedish gender equality politics; there has been a tendency to focus on 'the problems men experience' rather than 'the problems men cause' (cf. Hearn and Pringle, 2006). In the field of Nordic and Swedish masculinity studies, this can also be discerned by the fact, for instance, that research conducted by male scholars on men's violence against women in Sweden (and indeed internationally) has been relatively scarce (Pringle, 2005; Balkmar, Iovanni and Pringle, 2009; Egeberg Holmgren, 2011).

This is not to say that there are elements of Swedish society that aren't helpful in engaging men, and many also mentioned positive aspects around having more formalised and developed gender equality standards:

A positive thing about Sweden is that we have got lots of policy statements about men's violence to women and national gender equality goals. Then you can at least use those standards all the time to get the police and other authorities to develop this, to become better. We have these goals, we have to work towards these goals, and that makes it a little bit legitimate to talk about these things with practitioners and people at a higher level. You always have this support and they can't say anything against that. So I think that we truly need like conventions on the international level of importance. It's also very important that we have gender equality goals and that we have mission statements that agencies should do this, and that they have to follow up. Some countries where I've been working, they don't use a system of goals. On the other hand, we have the problem in Sweden of course that the issue of men's violence to women is not a professionalised question here. There are not so many professionals specifically working with men's violence to women. We don't find this issue dealt with in many programs at universities. (Patrik, Sweden)

Another man emphasised that parental leave provision in Sweden may mark a major change in men's behaviour, and believed this could have a long-term impact on levels of gendered violence. The idea to increase men's parental leave as a way to enhance gender equality, developing traits among men such as 'emotional competence' and making them less inclined to use violence against women and children, has long been part of the gender equality politics, sometimes referred to as 'daddy-politics' (Klinth and Johansson, 2010). In 2019, for the first time fathers used more than 30 per cent of the total number of yearly parental leave days ('Försäkringskassan' – Swedish Social Insurance Agency, 2019). At the same time, scholars have pointed out that 'child orientated masculinities' might not always be equivalent to gender equal oriented masculinities (Bekkengen, 2002) and when it comes to fathers' use of violence towards mothers the discourse has proved to be problematic (Eriksson, 2003).

Issues of parental leave were not reflected to the same extent in the other countries we looked at. In the UK there was thought to have been a shift in men's involvement in fatherhood, although this was a gradual one, and some organisations now have progressive policies with some elements of shared parental leave being allowed. There had historically been little pressure in Spain from men seeking to increase their participation in parental leave despite the significant changes in gender relations over recent generations. However, with Sweden playing a major influence in Spanish activism and policy in this regard, this has changed in the last decade, and greater equality in terms of paternity and maternity leave is planned from 2021.

Connected to this, some interviewees felt that there were particular events in a man's life that could represent pivotal opportunities to engage with them about taking a public stand against violence towards women, such as when they become a father:

Then, there are parents. I know many friends where having children kind of shakes their world and turns it upside down. So, I think that we also need men to open themselves up for that, to open themselves up to weakness. And to be in love is also to show yourself. (Patrik, Sweden)

As this quote illustrates, experiences such as becoming a parent can, at least temporarily, leave men more emotionally and philosophically open to embracing new ways of being, and to moving away from some harmful aspects of masculinity.

Limited political leadership

In the survey, 45 per cent strongly agreed and 40 per cent agreed that there was a need for a clear government statement of why men should be involved. There was some variation in the interviews in terms of to what extent this was happening in different countries at present.

Virtually none of the Swedish interviewees suggested that there was a need for the Swedish government to give a stronger social message about challenging sexism or men's violence against women. One reason for this may be revealed in what the following participant says about the ubiquity of a gender equality discourse in Swedish society, even among politicians:

In relation to [the possibilities off making radical change in Sweden] is when they said that all the government ministers in Sweden are gender equality ministers now. I understand the idea of gender mainstreaming. But when you start out with saying 'all ministers are gender equality ministers', you just hide it. And at the same time it's like, 'look at us', you know, 'here we are shining, everybody takes responsibility for gender inequality', so that means that nobody does. (Patrik, Sweden)

In Sweden, many mainstream politicians, including men, publicly define themselves as 'feminists'. What this means in practice is highly debatable, as our participant also implies. Nevertheless, the fact that the discourse of gender equality permeates Swedish politics so extensively does have consequences, as we noted above: some are positive and some less so. One consequence is that no one in Sweden doubts that men should be against violence towards women. Unfortunately, as we also noted earlier, the continued occurrence of men's violence against women in Sweden suggest there is a huge gap in the country between the ubiquity of a strong gender equality discourse and the reality of many Swedish women's lives. Another interviewee suggested we need to equip men in power not only with rhetoric, but also with knowledge – including practical knowledge – of how to make change. Finally, and crucially, several participants emphasised the need for men to not just take a public stance, but to also change themselves in order not to reproduce patriarchal structures.

The increase in right-wing and not always women-friendly attitudes in Swedish politics was discussed in Chapter 3. Some related issues were mentioned by participants. One interviewee described the state and politics (in particular when it has been social democratic/left leaning) in Sweden as being positive towards the preventive work being done. But those projects which do exist for preventing violence are under-funded. The economic crisis also concerned a number of participants. There were mixed responses to this. One expressed the view that there is a danger that economic problems and the social hardship caused by them may produce a 'nostalgic masculinity' which looks backwards. However, some of the other interviewees adopted more optimistic perspectives. A related issue which may affect men's anti-violence against women work, raised by some participants, is that the existing funding for much of this preventive work is already problematic. There are scarce resources to fund established projects, since most funding sources prioritise new development projects.

From the Spanish interviews, some political leaders who take a lead in challenging violence against women were highlighted. One who stood out in this respect was the Mayor of Barcelona, Ada Colau, under whom some actions to curb gender violence as part of a wider set of gender-equality measures for Barcelona had been taken. One example of this is increased monitoring of public spaces at night. The view of some interviewees was that men hold the power, but they don't think tackling violence against women is important. However, among male politicians, Pedro Zerolo, an important LGBTQ+ activist who died in 2015, was highlighted as having been especially supportive. Another example is Miguel Lorente Acosta (2009) who, in his role as the Delegate of the Spanish Government Against Gender Violence, implements and manages the laws of 2004 and 2007 against violence against women and equality of opportunities between men and women.

Where action was being taken against violence against women, it was largely by women's organisations, which had developed independently after the period of the Franco dictatorship. The 'Instituto de la Mujer' (Institute for Women) at the state level, and in each of the

Autonomous Communities, gained some funding and played an active, fundamental role in this regard (Bustelo, 2016). In contrast, more than one interviewee indicated there were very few resources to develop work with men in this field, and little pressure for this to happen. This was to a large extent a by-product of lack of support from institutions:

> For me an important thing is we don't have support from the institutions. And if you don't have support, it's not for money only – even more things than money. If you don't have this kind of support you can't make programmes – your impact in society is very small. (Pablo, Spain)

The only governmental institution specifically highlighted in this regard was the Catalan regional government: 'Here they are doing some activities, they are encouraging young NGOs and young associations, giving some resources, investing into the gender programmes' (Juan, Spain). Another interviewee felt that nowadays 'gesture politics' was all-pervasive, and provided an obstacle to real action being taken:

> You can make as many public statements as you want, make as many signs as you want, but there have to be resources to create changes. What has happened is we don't have resources any more, we have gesture politics, it's not being translated into programmes. (Didac, Spain)

However, one national initiative, the Pacto de Estado contra la Violencia de Género (National Pact against Gender Violence) was highlighted by one of the Spanish interviewees. This is a proposal that the feminist movement put on the political agenda, the objective being that all parties should make the fight against gender violence a government priority; it gained cross-party parliamentary approval in September 2017. This move marks a first step towards closing a huge inconsistency in existing Spanish legislation, whereby murders of women and their children are defined as gender violence only when the homicide is carried out by the woman's current or former partner, effectively restricting the definition of gender violence to domestic abuse – the law was changed in 2020. Although the interviewee was supportive of the initiative, he was disappointed that:

> They have concentrated on punishment and measures after the problem has emerged, and do not talk about working

> with men at all... I think that is a big mistake, because punishment doesn't change anything. (Jon, Spain)

Jon was hoping instead that the outcome would address not only male abusers, but prevention work too, and men more broadly in society.

The economic crisis in Spain (and wider Europe) in the years since 2008 has led to significant hardship. It was suggested by some of the Spanish interviewees that an enduring attachment among many men to the breadwinner ethos, together with the rise of more precarious work, might be connected in some ways to the perpetration of violence against women. In addition, the crisis may have affected whether men are likely to take a public stance on violence against women.

Similar to Sweden and Spain, a key political and economic issue which was raised by several of the British interviewees was the lack of funding for efforts to tackle men's violence against women in the UK, which was often connected to the UK government's wider austerity programme following the 2008 recession. It was felt that this was constraining the potential for organised efforts to prevent violence against women and engage with men and boys to grow, and was thus inhibiting opportunities for more men to take action:

> The current political situation is not conducive at all, and never has been. A lot of the issues are around funding. Even though the current government has talked a lot about domestic abuse, and is introducing legislative change and things, it is very slow. The Istanbul Convention has had a positive impact, however there is still a significant lack of understanding of the issues in the political sphere, which has an impact on funding. There have been massive cuts to funding, which creates a hostile environment. Services are becoming more competitive with each other, which has a detrimental impact on the services themselves – there are reduced services and fewer staff are having to do more with less. (Matthew, UK)

One interviewee reasoned that a form of more direct communication from political leadership would be of help:

> If there was a government policy specifically about men's violence against women, encouraging men to take a public stance against men's violence against women, that might help. Because it comes from the top down. If we could have

some leadership. If we could have some high-profile men, sports stars, actors, talking alongside the government, then I think we could get more men coming forward. Because they may have seen women being abused. So, if other men are able to identify non-physical forms of violence and abuse as well, then they might want to be part of that movement. Because if we don't see that, it's not going to happen. [...] So, I think a direct route led by government including celebrities, to recruit more men on violence against women initiatives. (Abbas, UK)

In our survey, there was agreement about the importance of involving celebrities in speaking out against violence against women (33 per cent strongly agreed, 44 per cent agreed) and for leadership figures in local communities and in settings such as sport or religion to speak out (60 per cent strongly agreed, 38 per cent agreed). This was expanded on by another UK interviewee who saw the type of man speaking out publicly as significant:

To generate this critical mass, we need men speaking out who are considered traditionally masculine and successful within that paradigm yet still calling it out – men such as Terry Crews [a former American football player, now an actor, who speaks out about the abuse his family experienced at the hands of his father] for example. This jarring contradiction will make other men realise that even if someone who seems to be 'winning' with conventional gendered norms has problems with them, then it makes us much more reflective and breaks that invisible hold gendered norms have over our behaviours as men. (Luke, UK)

One participant pointed out that the situation could be exacerbated by Britain's departure from the European Union, which they felt could add to the detrimental impacts upon government funding for violence against women services, as well as creating more poverty, which disproportionately affects women and children. He therefore felt that one of the biggest things that men taking a public stance could do would be to call for improved funding and increased provision of services for women and girls.

Connected to this, some of the interviewees also believed that there remains a lack of willpower from government and policymakers for preventing violence against women in the UK, even if they might make strong statements about the issue.

> It would help if the, whoever was the most senior politician in the parliament, whether it's Nicola Sturgeon in Scotland, or Boris Johnson in London, had to make a statement every year, about what their government was doing around gender-based violence, could be... it's whether or not, governments had a senior cabinet role around gender-based violence, or around, maybe not gender-based violence, but whoever had the portfolio for issues around equality, was seen as a much more, high profile, and senior appointment. Politicians would maybe, take more interest in it, because there's the natural sort of sense of, advancement. I think it would also be good if, probably with the media, that whenever they were looking for, people to comment on issues of gender-based violence, that certainly, it's not to say that they should be picking a man instead of a woman, but alongside a woman commentating on it, also work really hard to have a man who, is able to offer some commentary or viewpoint on it. So yeah, maybe it's news organisations actively always trying to and ensure that they are saying this is a men's issue as much as a women's issue. (Christopher, UK)

One participant argued that politicians often do not take the violence against women sector seriously, and that it is rarely at the top at the list of their priorities compared to issues such as terrorism. Another felt that when leading male British politicians do talk about gender inequality and violence against women, it is typically in very limited ways. He noted that there is a small minority of male politicians who do speak out about violence against women, but that they generally receive much less coverage and attention than men in politics who promote a 'backlash' towards feminism:

> I suspect that the media don't help. I don't think they want to hear men talking about this stuff, so they don't report it. So, they are much more likely to give some airtime to Phillip Davies [an MP who is renowned for expressing anti-feminist views] than to Gavin Newlands [an MP who is a public supporter of the White Ribbon campaign]. (Dean, UK)

One interviewee contended that while most British politicians would support campaigns to end violence against women, this would typically represent superficial support rather than a deeper commitment to tackling the problem, and it would be even rarer for this to include an emphasis on men's role in its prevention:

> Politicians are mostly supportive, you rarely get a negative response, although one did say to me that it 'never happens' in his area... but everyone is happy to have their photo taken and say, 'oh yes, of course I support this', but it's mostly tokenistic support. (Iain, UK)

However, he felt that if the UK government does ratify the Council of Europe's Istanbul Convention on preventing and combating violence against women and domestic violence, this could help to change the political agenda, as it does feature an emphasis on prevention, including a requirement to engage men and boys in this. This was not agreed upon by all in the survey however, where a relatively large proportion of respondents weren't sure that implementing the Istanbul Convention would make it easier for more men to speak out about violence against women (25 per cent didn't know, though 45 per cent still strongly agreed and 30 per cent agreed this was important). One respondent was particularly critical of the Istanbul Convention, writing: 'Don't believe in "conventions" from the same institutions and authorities that never address mainstream policies, and lock gender in a very narrow policy closet' (Spain).

Generally speaking, interviewees appeared to feel somewhat dispirited about the current political situation in the UK and the implications of that for efforts to prevent violence against women. Furthermore, one participant argued that it cannot be assumed that someone's specific political beliefs will mean they will actively oppose men's violence, and that there are men who are more and less supportive of ending gender-based violence across the political spectrum:

> Each political party has more and less progressive and profeminist men. One cannot assume that, because of espoused political beliefs, that you will actively work for social justice, and specifically with regards to ending men's violence against women. (Robert, UK)

However, at the same time, Robert also felt that the experience of collective struggle together with women, for example through trade unionism, could enable men to gain more of an insight into women's experiences of oppression, and in turn provide an impetus for change:

> No one socio-economic condition would make it more likely to be interested or active in tackling men's violence against women. However, the more privileged you are, the less reflective you tend to be. If a man is involved in some kind of collective struggle, such as through a trade union, with women, and listens to them about their experiences, that should provide some impetus to become more active. (Robert, UK)

Yet he also felt that political notions of solidarity in the UK are themselves being weakened:

> The workplace therefore should be – but the workplace is constantly changing, and solidarity is actively discouraged in it. Common empathetic struggle is discouraged in Britain today – the public sector is under attack, and there has been a weakening of the trade union movement. The basis has to be a common recognition of the full humanity of women by men. But that could be achieved in a vast array of contexts – we shouldn't focus on any one in particular. (Robert, UK)

Some of the interviewees argued that politics and political organisations can often be quite male-dominated, 'macho' environments, including within left-wing politics despite its emphasis on equality, with few men paying significant attention to issues connected with women's empowerment:

> I have heard about inappropriate behaviour even within socialist-leaning organisations, and it makes you wonder, why is no one calling these people out? Many left-wing organisations have traditionally been very male dominated... and were not addressing gender issues at all. This is still the case today – they still often fail to see how the personal is political. (Iain, UK)

At a broader level, some of the UK participants also referred to the influence of Donald Trump beyond the US, in normalising sexism and violence against women and encouraging the condoning of it within politics. However, it was suggested that Trump's election had also had an opposite effect in some ways, in that it had sparked considerable protest and resistance towards his sexist and misogynistic attitudes and behaviours:

> Trump is not in the UK, Sweden or Spain but he's still part of our public discourse. In some ways that's both conducive and not conducive. He's a very bad role model, but people are kicking against what he does, so there's more talk about it. (Iain, UK)

It was pointed out that Trump's election has consequently led to the development of new social movements and provided new opportunities to speak out about men's violence against women, compelling more men to take a public stance against it in the process.

'Not all men are bastards' – changing the language?

A few of the participants felt that some of the language and focus of talking to men and boys about violence against women and girls had to change in order to bring a broader group of people on board with the topic. This is undoubtably a controversial argument to make. One of the Spanish participants for example felt that one way of doing this was to use words such as 'equality' more than words such as 'feminism' – the latter which may invoke particularly strong feelings and stereotypes.

> I think we need to change the kind of, one of the actions is change the word, for example most men are afraid of the word feminism, we could change it to another word. We try to change the language, we can do more positive things. Because the first time it's like a word that makes men afraid. But we change it, we can involve men to participate too. (Juan, Spain)

In the UK, Abbas felt that we needed to go even further than this, particularly if education and awareness raising were to enter much broader spaces such as religious settings and places of worship:

> There needs to be an element of stop blaming men for men's violence against women, because not all men are like this. I accept that men are the problem, but I also think men are part of the solution. Forgive me for saying this, but if we

are to make positive inroads into particular organisations like mosques then we need men involved. (Abbas, UK)

The 'not all men' argument has (justifiably) become highly controversial and heavily criticised, because it can be seen as excusing men for inaction in relation to a problem which affects everyone in society, and ignores the various ways in which men are complicit in violence against women and patriarchy (such as through wider sexist and misogynistic attitudes and behaviours) (Castelino, 2014). In Sweden, the 'not all men' argument has been used in comic strips to illustrate the sensitivity often shown as soon as 'men are named as men'. However, it could be argued from Abbas' comments that further consideration and discussion is still needed about how to effectively communicate messages about men's violence against women to different populations of men and boys.

This idea of making involvement somehow less confrontational for men was also one put forward by Lee:

> I think it might help men to understand how they can navigate the language of feminism, should they say they are a feminist or an ally of feminism, making it easier, and there's a risk of what it can mean, I tell you now, I sometimes despair when I see the language of my way or the highway, if you don't say this then you're not with us, and I think some of this is sounding really fundamentalist. I don't sit easy with movements that are very black and white and you have to sign up to this. We need to have the ambiguousness about it, without getting beaten up, why can't I help the feminist cause and do some good things while not being a woman. I understand why women are very angry, not as well as they do, but I do get some of the things. But not all men are bastards, and many men don't know how to help. I don't think men can be free while women are in jail in terms of life. While we are in theory free we have to jail you, that doesn't sound to me like real freedom. Real freedom is that that gives everything away, so everyone else can be free too. (Lee, UK)

Similarly, for Robert, the tone of content which seeks to prepare men to take action was important:

The availability of reasonable, intelligent, respectful but challenging information, voices, and discourse, that they can read and say 'yes, I get that, I'm not being hectored, but it is asking something of me, it is hard hitting'. A positive presence that puts forward the case clearly, and allows men to feel ready to do so – bringing people to the point of readiness to change – you have to want to change (which you can only get to through a tough reflective process). (Robert, UK)

One respondent, feeling pessimistic about the (low) levels of knowledge among many men in positions of power, argued that work against men's violence needs to locate these men 'where they are at', even if it means appealing to their self-interest:

Unfortunately, one should say, the way society looks, it is not enough to motivate men that women are subjected to violence. [...] I know, it's totally damn sick, that that isn't good enough. It's crazy. But I believe... then you have to, I think make sure that there is... you know, using strategies where there is self-interest for men, or interest in the children. I've seen those studies, that when you need to make men using violence to stop, it doesn't work to talk about what it is doing to his partner, or what it does to him. He's beyond that, no care of self either. But when it comes to what this does to the children, there is a specific chink in the armour reaching some kind of empathy. That 'oh, ok', when they hear how this affects the children. So I believe, I guess... then we'll use that. If that is, like, the chink in the armour that patriarchy has to offer. (Kristian, Sweden)

This was also mentioned in the survey, where one respondent suggested:

I think articulating the benefits to men of gender equality is key, in addition to educating men on the reality of what that inequality looks like and how it impacts on women that they care about in their lives. (UK)

Burrell (2018) has argued in relation to these debates that the way forward may be to seek a balance between appealing to men with a positive message which they can relate to, while also challenging them about their complicity in patriarchy and encouraging them to create change, both within themselves and in wider society. Furthermore, while it is vital to find effective ways of reaching out to men, it is important to ensure that the profeminist principles of anti-violence work with men and boys are not overly compromised in the process, or else the driving force of the work will become lost.

#MeToo

In 2017, longstanding efforts to end sexual violence reached a new level as the #MeToo movement hit the global stage. It was first initiated as a campaign against sexual violence and in solidarity with survivors by feminist activist and community organiser Tarana Burke in the United States in 2006 (Fileborn and Loney-Howes, 2019). It then rose to global prominence through social media in October 2017 when the actor Alyssa Milano encouraged women to say 'me too' if they had experienced some form of sexual violence in the wake of numerous allegations of sexual abuse being made against Harvey Weinstein in the US, and the hashtag became popularly used (Boyle, 2019; McKinney, 2019). These events overlapped with the period in which we were carrying out our data collection (November–December 2017), and the #MeToo movement had a significant impact on many European countries, although this did vary substantially in different contexts.

We asked survey respondents whether #MeToo had highlighted sexual harassment and encouraged more men to speak out about violence against women in their country, and 21 per strongly agreed and 54 per agreed that it had. However, this was the question in the survey that saw the greatest difference between countries – men in Sweden were far more likely to agree with this statement than men in Spain or the UK.

All of the Swedish survey participants either agreed (60 per cent) or strongly agreed (40 per cent that #MeToo had highlighted sexual harassment and encouraged more men to speak out. This compares to the UK where just under three quarters (74 per cent) of men either agreed (64 per cent) or strongly agreed (9 per cent) and Spain where less than two thirds (61 per cent) either agreed (44 per cent) or strongly agreed (17 per cent) with the statement. These national differences in results might reflect that the #MeToo movement became much stronger in Sweden than in many other European countries and had a greater impact both in terms of public and political debates. This also impacted activism, including initiatives taken by organisations and gender equality projects involving men (see for instance the #guytalk and #killmiddag initiative discussed in Chapter 3).

The #MeToo movement had a prominent impact within the Swedish media, across social media as well as traditional news coverage. Moreover, more than 50 campaigns dedicated to specific industries, professions or sectors posed a significant number of challenges to politicians and employers to take action against sexual harassment and gendered violence. The sector of culture, media and art workers aside, campaigns were created in a wide range of fields, from ex-offender women battling substance abuse and women in the sex industry, to women in the forestry sector. It has been suggested that this aspect of #MeToo makes Sweden stand out in an international perspective (Johansson, Johansson and Andersson, 2018).

It is interesting to note that a sizeable proportion of respondents, 18 per cent across all three countries, weren't sure about the impact of the movement on men, suggesting that we may only know in the longer term about the extent to which #MeToo has helped to create serious, lasting social change in terms of preventing men's violence against women. This was particularly the case among Spanish respondents, with 33 per cent replying that they didn't know.

This is perhaps unsurprising, given that Spain has had its own, slightly different version of #MeToo which arose later, based around the hashtag #Cuéntalo ('tell it'). This was initiated to express solidarity with the victim of a gang rape that was perpetrated at Pamplona's San Fermín festival in 2016, after the five-month trial of this case ended in April 2018. The five men involved (who called themselves La Manada – 'The Wolf Pack'), one of whom was an officer in the Spanish Civil Guard, were cleared of sexual assault and charged with the lesser crime of sexual abuse, with each being sentenced to nine years in prison. The acquittal of the men for sexual assault led to mass outrage in Spain and waves of protests involving hundreds of thousands of people (mainly women but also men) across the country (Abrisketa and Abrisketa, 2020). Earlier that year, millions of women had also taken part in a 'feminist strike' on International Women's Day in protest against ongoing gender inequality (Campillo, 2019). The differing situation in Spain was reflected in the survey responses about #MeToo, with one writing: 'The campaign is only just reaching Spain (with quite a delay) and is being translated/adapted. Not too many men have made public statements yet.' Another simply wrote that 'Spain is a macho place'. One Spanish participant even responded that he was unaware of the #MeToo campaign.

A range of other responses were given to this question. Many of the respondents appeared to feel that #MeToo had a particularly sizeable impact in terms of women's voices being heard and awareness being raised about sexual violence and harassment. For instance, one wrote 'this campaign has helped to break the silence on the issue of sexual harassment against women' (Spain). Another commented that 'I think it has given a platform of confidence which is great. Strength in numbers' (UK), while one felt that it had led to 'geater awareness and visibility of the problem of violence against women by men' (Spain).

This again points to how specific and particularly shocking cases (or cases in which there is a particularly shocking response from the state), such as that of 'The Wolf Pack' which receive widespread media coverage, can break through into the public imagination, and provide deeper insights into the pervasiveness of men's violence against women in society. In turn this, and the social mobilisations and protests it can provoke (particularly among feminist movements), can lead more men to question their relationship with violence and abuse, and motivate some to start taking a public stance against it.

However, several appeared to feel that by comparison, men had remained relatively silent and passive in relation to #MeToo and related movements. For instance, one UK participant wrote: 'I think that the campaign has largely been about women talking about their experiences. Men have largely been observers, for various reasons, or some men have come out to criticize or attack the campaign.' Another commented that 'I haven't heard men speaking out more since the Me Too campaign' (UK), while one pointed out that 'I haven't noticed this campaign reach people outside of some critical streams' (Spain).

Other respondents were more optimistic about the influences that #MeToo had on men. For example, one wrote that it had 'engaged many men and women in conversations about this issue that previously might not have happened' (UK). Another commented: 'I think that awareness of the pervasiveness of VAWG [violence against women and girls] is the first step for any man interested in getting involved' (UK), while one noted that 'I have seen more men openly stand against VAW in social media' (Spain). However, one respondent also underlined the importance of being cautious about men's involvement in feminist-led movements such as #MeToo, and that sometimes men's interventions in relation to it had been questionable:

> I think that's true, but there has also been an unhelpful response from men joining in in using the hashtag. Whilst many of us have experienced sexual abuse and/

or harassment it's far from the same and such responses must feel insulting and dispiriting to women. Men must acknowledge our privilege and power if we are to become allies. (UK)

This point does raise challenging questions about where men's own experiences of violence and abuse fit in relation to movements against violence against women. Can the voices of male victim-survivors bolster such movements and highlight the pervasiveness of violence and abuse (especially that perpetrated by men) across society? Or does this risk detracting from the focus on the specific gendered dynamics of men's violence against women, and women's struggles for liberation? On the other hand, it could also compound feelings of powerlessness and isolation if male victim-survivors feel like they are not 'permitted' to speak out about their experiences as part of such movements. This highlights the importance of men providing more support for one another as one way of avoiding 'taking over' or delegitimising women's spaces and movements, including in relation to men's own experiences of violence and abuse within patriarchy.

We also asked the survey respondents what they felt the most important actions were that individual men could take to support women speaking out about experiences of violence and abuse through campaigns such as #MeToo.

Again, all of the actions we suggested were strongly backed by the respondents, demonstrating the wide range of impactful things that men can do to support women who are speaking out about men's violence. The action which received the highest level of agreement of all was supporting women when you witness violence or harassment (90 per cent strongly agreed, 10 per cent agreed). However, two UK respondents provided important qualifications about this, with one writing: 'This has to be done with care and empathy, to avoid either increasing risk or being condescending, or self-serving. Knights in shining armour are not helpful!' and another similarly stating, 'In relation to the last point, supporting women is important, but only works if the man attempting to do so understands how and the wider context of the system in which VAWG operates, i.e. no saviour complex.' This underlines how vital it is for men to think carefully when they are seeking to take steps to support women's efforts against men's violence, and reflect on their motivations for doing so to ensure they are not inadvertently reproducing unequal power dynamics in the process, or perhaps even making the problem worse (Murphy, 2009).

Figure 5: The most important actions men can take to support women speaking out through campaigns such as #MeToo, n = 40

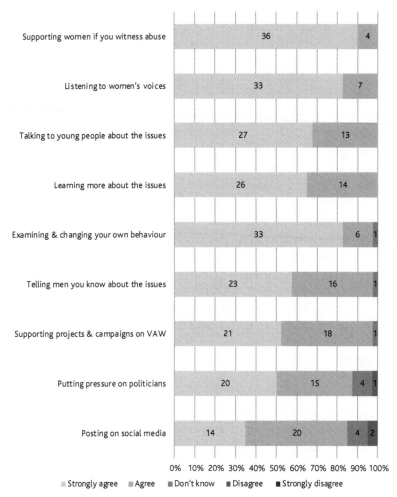

Other actions which received particularly high levels of support among respondents were: listening to women's voices (83 per cent strongly agreed, 17 per cent agreed); examining and changing your own behaviour towards women (83 per cent strongly agreed, 15 per cent agreed); talking to young people about the issues (68 per cent strongly agreed, 32 per cent agreed); and learning about the issues (65 per cent strongly agreed, 35 per cent agreed). There was very little disagreement with any of the suggested actions, although 5 per cent disagreed and 10 per cent were unsure about posting on social media to defend women's right to live free from violence (while 50 per cent agreed and 35 per cent strongly agreed), and 3 per cent disagreed and 10 per cent were unsure about putting pressure on politicians at European, national and local levels, perhaps demonstrating there being slightly more scepticism about the impact that these two actions can have.

Summary

This chapter has considered how best to move on from male activists on violence against women being an 'untypical minority' (Christian, 1994: 4), making it a more common form of work or activism for men in the future. There was quite a lot of agreement between our participants that men working in NGOs, men who were already involved in other social justice movements, and men who themselves had faced particular forms of discrimination were more likely to be involved in speaking out about men's violence against women. Higher education was noted as a context which was seen as particularly conducive to men being involved, just as it was important in terms of men's routes into activism as discussed in Chapter 2. However, even within these groups and contexts there is still only a minority of men involved. The quest therefore is both to increase involvement within these groups where there are already a small number of men who are active, and also to look to areas where there is a smaller proportion of men involved, for example among wealthier men, men in right-leaning political groups or men in positions of power. This is not to ignore that there are also definite risks to involving more men – whether from particular groups or more generally.

Education, knowledge and awareness were agreed upon as being absolutely central both to ending violence against women generally and in terms of specifically increasing men's involvement in activism to end violence against women. Although a lot of the focus was on pre-school and school level education, workplace education and wider approaches to spreading knowledge such as through the media were also highlighted as important. Religious institutions were seen as one place that had been overlooked in terms of engagement and education. Working class men were argued by some as being overlooked and perhaps also facing more obstacles to taking action against gender-based inequalities, while also potentially being able to feel a sense of solidarity with women's struggles by connecting them with their own experiences of oppression.

A number of obstacles, or factors that might prevent men from taking action, were explored. As well as those we asked about in the survey, such as seeing violence against women as a 'woman's issue' and a lack of interest or motivation, others emerged through the free text comments in the survey and through the interviews. Ironically, having a strong gender equality discourse which might be seen as an opportunity was also cast as a challenge, particularly in Sweden. A stronger political leadership was seen as more necessary in the UK and Spain than in Sweden. Austerity politics following the 2008 recession was also identified as a significant barrier, and there were concerns raised that the UK leaving the European Union would bring with it additional detrimental shifts.

Finally, we explored the impact of #MeToo. In Chapter 2 we talked about the impact of how, on an individual level, experiences of violence and abuse close to men could have the impact of 'catapulting' them into the area of violence against women prevention. High profile, particularly 'shocking' cases could represent significant moments in other men's journeys to become more involved. It was clear that while #MeToo had a huge impact in Sweden, the impact of this was less pronounced in the UK and Spain. For Spain, their national version of #MeToo was linked to a high-profile rape trial which resulted in organising around '#Cuéntalo' ('tell it').

5

Conclusions: where next?

Knowing how prevalent violence against women and girls is in society and the devastation it causes, it is our contention that more people – men and boys included – need to play a part in the struggle to reduce and ultimately end it. This means not only being an equal and non-violent partner in interpersonal, family and work lives, but also being willing to speak out publicly – to challenge and take a public stance against violence against women. This is controversial in some ways, not least because of some of the obstacles identified in this book. On the one hand, men may be 'put on a pedestal', potentially taking praise for work and ideas initiated by women. Some men involved in anti-violence against women work have themselves used violence, abuse or harassment against women. On the other hand, this research has shown that being a man speaking publicly on this topic is not without risks and struggles. It can be difficult for men to join friendship groups with other men involved in this work. However, they can simultaneously find it difficult to join in more traditional men's friendship groups because they can be seen as 'different' or 'argumentative' (for example if they challenge sexist jokes). Just as 'hate' mail – be it online or offline – is frequently experienced by women who work in this field (Lewis, Rowe and Wiper, 2017), this research has shown that men may also be on the receiving end of hatred from other men in relation to their public stance against men's violence against women.

The objectives of this book were to explore the personal backgrounds and life experiences associated with men moving to positions where they actively and publicly challenge men's violence in society and also to consider the structures and cultural and social norms that might be conducive to enabling and supporting more men to do so. In some ways this book provides an additional lens to support what previous research (as described in Chapter 1) has found in other contexts: the importance of formative experiences which challenge masculine expectations; the influence of women in men's lives; the relevance of professional pathways; the influence of involvement in other progressive movements and struggles; the tensions accompanying men's involvement; and the need to engage further with men and boys in the quest to end violence against women. In other ways, we offer new contributions to the field and, inevitably, in doing so open up a plethora of new questions requiring investigation in future research.

Supporting research by others

Our findings about how the men we spoke to were influenced to become involved was similar to previous research in some ways. Experiences such as not conforming to dominant notions of masculinity when growing up, becoming a father and coming into contact with feminist ideas at university were significant for many of our participants. The men's diverse routes into anti-violence activism also demonstrate the importance of an intersectional approach to understanding these pathways to understand formative experiences which challenge masculine expectations (Peretz, 2017).

Most significant of all was the fundamental role played by feminist women, both by directly or indirectly encouraging participants to get involved in efforts to end violence against women, and then by supporting them after they became involved. By contrast, other men often appeared to play a small or negative role in participants' lives. Previous research has found similar things about the influence that feminist women such as mothers and partners can have on men. However, it also challenges the assumption that men 'will only listen to other men' or that 'male role models' are essential (see also Ruxton et al, 2019).

Another key influence for some of our participants in becoming involved in anti-violence activism was their professional lives. This chimes with Messner, Greenberg and Peretz's (2015) finding that the work of male allies to end violence against women is becoming increasingly professionalised. Our research demonstrates that professional experiences (including in workplaces broader than gender equality work specifically) appear to be playing an increasing role in fostering men's pathways towards anti-violence activism, which has a number of implications. For example, it could mean that men participating in such efforts are coming from more diverse backgrounds, experiences and perspectives, and having more of a practical focus, but also that their work may be less rooted in or informed by feminist theory and activism. It also illustrates the value of engaging men in discussions about violence against women in the workplace, for example through training and awareness-raising campaigns.

Our research found additional evidence of some of the tensions that can arise when men become involved in the feminist-led movement to end violence against women. For example, the 'pedestal effect' described by Messner, Greenberg and Peretz (2015) and the problems associated with men 'talking the talk but not walking the walk'. It also showed some of the ways in which men can act to address and reduce these potential problems (for instance, by continuously engaging in critical self-reflection, and elevating the work done by women), demonstrating that while some tensions may be inherent to this work, they do not make it any less important.

Finally, many of our participants re-emphasised the need to engage with and educate men and boys much more about violence and abuse, masculinity, and gender equality issues, most urgently at school and in higher education, but also in society more broadly, such as in the workplace. This would significantly help efforts to prevent men's violence against women from happening in the first place, and could also encourage more men to take a public stance against it.

New contributions to the field

Our findings bring important new knowledge to the field in a number of areas, with a multi-country, European lens. The majority of research in this field to date has come from a North American perspective, and there are important differences in relation to issues such as different welfare regimes, responses to the 2007 financial crash, and the nature and forms of racism in Europe, which all impact on efforts to end violence against women. The study of men and masculinities from a transnational, European perspective can bring with it important new insights, as Hearn and Pringle (2006) have demonstrated.

One area in which our findings provide new insights is in highlighting the difference between men who begin taking action as a gradual process (which was the case for most of the men in our research) and those for whom there is a specific event which inspires them to get involved in anti-violence work. For example, as a result of the homicide of a family member, or hearing about, witnessing or experiencing other specific acts of men's violence. Our research has demonstrated that while specific 'moments' and 'events' can undoubtedly be important, for many men who become involved in activism to end violence against women, they reach this point through a gradual process which can involve a range of different factors. These may include their upbringing, their experiences at school, university and in the workplace, and structural issues such as their social positions and interactions with power and privilege. It therefore seems to be key to put in place as many positive 'prompts' as possible along the life course to encourage men along a path towards feminism and anti-violence.

At the same time, for a minority of the men we spoke to, it was a specific event which 'catapulted' them into anti-violence work, even if there may still have been other factors over the course of their lives which influenced this. This was typically the murder of women and/ or children in their lives (such as family members) by a man. Other research has shown that experiencing men's violence, either directly or indirectly (for example, by witnessing it, or hearing about another person's experiences) either as a one-off or a prolonged experience, has a significant influence on some men (eg Casey and Smith, 2010), and this was also the case for several of our participants. However, less discussed has been the impact that one event can have. Specific cases which receive significant national attention or which are especially shocking and harrowing can also have a major galvanising effect on society as a whole, including on some men, as was found with our Spanish interviewees in particular.

Our findings also highlight the importance of men supporting one another. While men generally appeared to have less influence than women on our participants initially, once they became involved relationships with other men in a variety of contexts often played a key role in supporting and sustaining that. This highlights the importance of men involved in anti-violence activism finding and building support networks with other men where possible. One of the benefits to this includes helping men to deal with some of the personal costs that can accompany being involved, such as feeling isolated. Another benefit is helping to hold one another accountable, so that less of this burden falls on women. At the same time, it's important to acknowledge that there can be risks associated with all-male groups and networks (such as failing to identify the persistence of patriarchal attitudes and behaviours, or focusing solely on issues which harm men), which also demonstrates the importance of continuing to listen to and learn from feminist activists, and building strong collaborative relationships with women's movement organisations.

Another important finding that our research highlights is the importance of context – settings conducive to men taking action – and how some settings can be more conducive than others for men to become involved in anti-violence activism. For example, 'not for profit' NGOs/voluntary/community organisations, progressive political groups and social welfare services were seen as being particularly important in this respect. This highlights where it might be most effective to target efforts to recruit more men into activism to end violence against women. It also raises the question of what makes some contexts more conducive than others, and what different approaches might be needed to engage more men in other settings, such as the police or local government, or in other political groupings. Music and sporting venues may also prove effective recruiting grounds, especially among younger men, as the work of organisations such as White Ribbon in the UK suggests.

Finally, several of our participants raised the dangers posed by anti-feminist, misogynistic groups such as 'men's rights activists', who appear to be recruiting increasing numbers of men in some countries, especially online through the so-called 'manosphere'. Since our research, this has been investigated in more depth in an important book by Bates (2020) on 'extreme misogyny'. This shows that men who become curious about and active on gender issues can go in a very different direction to that of our participants. Men in the anti-violence field can play a vital role in challenging these viewpoints, and this is arguably a more important area of focus for this work than ever – countering and providing an alternative to masculinist, 'macho', misogynistic politics.

Lessons for future research

The number of men actively involved in efforts to end violence against women in Spain, Sweden and the UK remains somewhat small. Although we believe this research to be the most extensive piece of work engaging with men in Europe to date, it is important to remember that the study was carried out with a relatively small sample of 64 men (24 interviews and 40 survey participants). There is a need to conduct more research with a more diverse group of men who challenge violence and dominant masculine norms in different countries, so that we can better understand the differences and similarities that exist in men's activism and learn lessons from different contexts.

The Black Lives Matter movement, which was reignited by the killing of George Floyd by police officers in the United States in May 2020, but has subsequently spread around the world, has shone a light on the extent to which racism and racial injustice remains structurally embedded in societies. Significant disparities exist in power and privilege among men based on intersecting social inequalities around race and ethnicity, as well as social class, sexuality, disability, age and more. A lot of the research on men and masculinities and men's activism to support feminist movements to date has not sufficiently recognised the differences in experiences and practices of men in different social groups, as has been highlighted by Peretz (2017). This has also been a gap in this study. We therefore need to think more deeply and more broadly about what 'men's anti-violence activism and work' looks like in future research. It's important to consider ways in which men are speaking out and taking action to stop violence and abuse and challenge dominant masculine norms which may be more marginalised, or which don't necessarily receive the same attention as more traditional, mainstream forms, such as those practiced by white, middle class men in arenas such as academia. Black Lives Matter poses vital questions about how we can make anti-violence activism, work and research more intersectional, more inclusive, and arguably more radical in the future.

In addition, our study highlighted the potential for reaching out to men who are already engaged in activism in relation to other social justice issues, such as environmental movements. There are also opportunities for cross-sectoral learning and exchange of effective practices and approaches in this regard. For example, groups such as Extinction Rebellion draw extensively on the non-violent methods associated with Mahatma Gandhi and Martin Luther King Jr. They also use the techniques of Non-Violent Communication (NVC) developed by Marshall Rosenberg (2015), foregrounding, among other things, recognition of shared needs, the importance of active listening and de-escalation skills, so as to avoid unintentional harm. They have engaged too in actions that draw attention to the relationship between care for oneself, care for others and care for the planet, and emphasise wellbeing at the heart of their 'regenerative culture' (Westwell and Bunting, 2020). Many of these features of the contemporary environmental movement can be seen as relevant to the development of men's anti-violence activism, and as being influenced by feminist theory and practice.

Our research emphasises the need for both a global and local perspective. Although there were undoubtably more difficulties and delays in conducting and writing up our research, mostly linked to language differences and different academic cultures and traditions (including the main writing and non-teaching times of the year), conducting transnational research offers vital opportunities for new insights. We learnt far more through these struggles and discussions than we would have alone, and more of this is needed in research on men's anti-violence activism in the future to enable shared learning and coalition-building internationally as well as nationally. Men's anti-violence activism is becoming increasingly global through transnational connections and networks such as the MenEngage Alliance and research needs to follow. From 2020, with large amounts of this work now taking place online as an impact of the COVID-19 pandemic, geographical boundaries are becoming more blurred than ever.

At the same time, the research also reveals the significant differences which exist in different countries in Europe, let alone across the wider world. Local and national contexts play a significant role in shaping anti-violence work; for example, differences in the dynamics of political contexts and how civil society is organised have significant implications. Furthermore, men's activism is at very different 'places' in different countries, and what is seen as being 'the norm' or an achievement in one country is not necessarily the same for another. For example, men playing an organisational role in marches and vigils to end violence against women would be a significant step forward in the UK, but in Spain these have already been happening for some time. The #MeToo movement created far more of an impact on men's work in Sweden (and other Nordic countries) than it did in the UK or Spain. It is therefore crucial to avoid over-generalising when discussing the nature of men's anti-violence activism in different countries.

What does the future look like for men's anti-violence activism?

The 'digital turn', and the implications of #MeToo and related movements, have been important and are likely to continue to be so. These have got more men thinking about the everyday nature of sexual violence and harassment, how they are implicated in it, and what they can do about it (eg listening to and supporting women who experience violence or harassment, talking to young people and other men and boys about these issues). In some countries (eg Spain, Sweden), they appear to have got a lot more men involved in some form of anti-violence activism. However, the long-term legacies of these movements remain unclear. In some ways they have significantly challenged men's violence against women in society and led to improvements in responses to it, as well as led to more perpetrators being held to account. Yet at the same time, men's violence appears to remain as pervasive as ever. There have been serious allegations of sexual violence made against very high-profile men who have still not faced any consequences for their actions (not least former President of the United States, Donald Trump). There is, therefore, an opportunity but also a danger of online activism that does not bring with it deeper, more radical social change.

Given the European focus of the research, it is important to consider the implications of the UK's departure from the European Union, which was voted for in 2017 and took place in January 2020, and has been an ongoing process throughout the duration of the project. Brexit can be seen as influenced by masculine approaches to politics, given its roots in ideas such as Britain being 'tough enough to go it alone', individualism and self-reliance rather than cooperation and mutual support. As a result, it has some overlaps with nationalist, xenophobic, right-wing populist and misogynistic political movements which are heavily influenced by masculinist politics and which have been gaining ground in some European countries in recent years (Greig, 2019). In addition, Brexit could undermine legislative change that has advanced gender equality in the UK and been brought in through the European Union, around issues such as equal pay, leave arrangements and health and safety at work. The economic fallout could also lead to deeper government austerity measures, which tend to disproportionately impact women, as they are more likely to work in and utilise public services.

Brexit could also be seen as being one part of wider global shifts away from international cooperation, as has been witnessed during the COVID-19 crisis, such as with nationalism around vaccines, the US withdrawing funds from the WHO and countries such as Poland and Turkey undermining and threatening to leave the Istanbul Convention. Again, this aversion towards international cooperation has been heavily influenced by 'macho' political leaders, and poses risks of increased tensions, posturing and conflict. Work to counter this through the building of European and internationally oriented collaborations, networks, activism and research is therefore vital.

It is therefore impossible to overlook the implications of the COVID-19 pandemic, which started on a global scale during spring 2020, despite it emerging just as we were finishing writing this book. In fact, the move to home schooling while attempting to continue with paid work, the loneliness, the anxiety, and the health fears brought about by coronavirus have had an impact on the writing of this book as they have undoubtedly had on many others.

On the one hand, the pandemic has created and deepened issues linked to ending violence against women, such as further entrenching social inequalities (for example, women in particular have been forced to take on increased caring responsibilities and have disproportionately been losing their jobs from the ensuing economic crisis). It has also exacerbated some harmful expressions of masculinity, such as men's use of violence and abuse against women and children at home or online. For example, all three countries in this study saw increased reports of violence against women and children during spring and summer 2020 (Hydén, 2020; UN Women, 2020). It could also lead some men to seek to revert to or protect patriarchal norms and privileges at a time when the status quo is being shaken – including politically, such as through the bolstering of reactionary, anti-feminist political forces in some contexts.

However, it has also created new opportunities for change: it has shone a new light on men's violence against women and children, and encouraged reflection and a new sense of perspective among some men (for example about the health and wellbeing of themselves and others). It has led (some) men to play a more active role in caregiving and community support, has demonstrated the significance of care and interconnectedness to society, created new ways of working (ie not in physical workplaces), reduced borders and barriers in some ways (eg due to more virtual meetings) and strengthened (international) activist networks online.

Final words

It was as we were putting the finishing touches to this book that many in the UK and further afield were shocked to hear that British woman Sarah Everard, a Durham University alumnus, had been kidnapped from a busy London street and found murdered shortly afterwards. A police officer was arrested and charged for these offences. Sarah Everard's murder resulted in a wave of public sadness and mourning, and also of anger and protests. For some, this has awoken a new or renewed sense of outrage and commitment to end men's violence against women in all its forms – indeed we have been contacted by men who are interested in joining or setting up campaigns for the first time. It remains to be seen whether this will lead to a surge of men becoming involved in anti-violence activism in the longer term.

The men who took part in our research demonstrate that violence against women is not inevitable and that men can and do defy dominant, patriarchal ideas of masculinity. We are grateful to the men who participated in our research, and to the women who pave the way and support men in their involvement. We continue to dream of and actively work towards creating a kinder future, free from violence and abuse. Men taking a public stance against violence against women is an important part of achieving this future.

References

Abrisketa, O.G. and Abrisketa, M.G. (2020) ' "It's okay, sister. Your wolf-pack is here": sisterhood as public feminism in Spain', *Signs*, 45(4): 931–53.

Almqvist, A.-L. and Duvander, A.-Z. (2014) 'Changes in gender equality? Swedish fathers' parental leave, division of childcare and housework', *Journal of Family Studies*, 20(1): 19–27.

Alonso, A. (2015) *El Mainstreaming de Género en España: Hacia un Compromiso Transversal con la Igualdad [Gender Mainstreaming in Spain: Towards a Commitment to Equality]*, Valencia: Tirant lo Blanch.

Azpiazu, J. (2017) *Masculinidades y Feminism [Masculinities and Feminism]*, Barcelona: Virus.

Bacete, R. (2017) *Nuevos Hombres Buenos: La Masculinidad en la Era del Feminismo [New Good Men: Masculinity in the Age of Feminism]*, Barcelona: Editorial Península.

Balkmar, D., Iovanni, L. and Pringle, K. (2009) 'A reconsideration of two "welfare paradises": research and policy responses to men's violence in Denmark and Sweden', *Men and Masculinities*, 12(2): 155–74.

Bambra, C. (2007) 'Going beyond the three worlds of welfare capitalism: regime theory and public health research', *Journal of Epidemiology and Community Health*, 61(12): 1098–102.

Bates, L. (2020) *Men Who Hate Women*, London: Simon & Schuster UK.

Bekkengen, L. (2002) *Man får välja: om föräldraskap och föräldraledighet i arbetsliv och familjeliv [Men Can Choose: Parenthood and Paternal Leave in Working and Family Life]*, Malmö: Liber Ekonomi.

Bonino, L. (2008) *Hombres y violencia de género. Más allá de los maltratadores y de los factores de riesgo [Men and gender violence: Beyond abusers and risk factors]*, Delegación de Gobierno para Violencia de Género [Government Delegation for Gender Violence], Madrid: Ministerio de Igualdad [Ministry of Equality], Available from: https://violenciagenero.igualdad.gob.es/violenciaEnCifras/estudios/colecciones/estudio/hombresYViolencia.htm [Accessed 28 March 2021].

Boyle, K. (2019) *#MeToo, Weinstein and Feminism*, Cham: Palgrave Macmillan.

Braun, V. and Clarke, V. (2006) 'Using thematic analysis in psychology', *Qualitative Research in Psychology*, 3(2): 77–101.

Bridges, T. (2010) 'Men just weren't made to do this: performances of drag at "walk a mile in her shoes" marches', *Gender and Society*, 24(1): 5–30.

Burrell, S.R. (2018) 'The contradictory possibilities of engaging men and boys in the prevention of men's violence against women in the UK', *Journal of Gender-Based Violence*, 2(3): 447–64.

Burrell, S.R. (2019) 'Engaging men and boys in the prevention of men's violence against women in England', Doctoral thesis, Durham, UK: Durham University.

Burrell, S.R. (2020) 'Male agents of change and disassociating from the problem in the prevention of violence against women', in R. Luyt and K. Starck (eds) *Masculine Power and Gender Equality: Masculinities as Change Agents*, Cham: Springer, pp 35–54.

Bustelo, M. (2016) 'Three decades of state feminism and gender equality policies in multi-governed Spain', *Sex Roles*, 74(3–4): 107–20.

Campillo, I. (2019) '"If we stop, the world stops": the 2018 feminist strike in Spain', *Social Movement Studies*, 18(2): 252–8.

Casey, E. and Smith, T. (2010) '"How can I not?": men's pathways to involvement in anti-violence against women work', *Violence against Women*, 16(8): 953–73.

Casey, E.A., Tolman, R.M., Carlson, J., Allen, C.T. and Storer, H.L. (2017) 'What motivates men's involvement in gender-based violence prevention? Latent class profiles and correlates in an international sample of men', *Men and Masculinities*, 20(3): 294–316.

Castelino, T. (2014) 'A feminist critique of men's violence against women efforts', *No To Violence Journal*, Autumn 2014: 7–14.

Christian, H. (1994) *The Making of Anti-Sexist Men*, London: Routledge.

Connell, R.W. (2005) *Masculinities* (2nd edn), Cambridge: Polity Press.

Coronado, N. (ed) (2017) *Hombres por la Igualdad [Men for Equality]*, Madrid: LoQueNoExiste.

Coulter, R.P. (2003) 'Boys doing good: young men and gender equity', *Educational Review*, 55(2): 135–45.

Delap, L. (2018) 'Feminism, masculinities and emotional politics in late twentieth century Britain', *Cultural and Social History*, 15(4): 571–93.

Delgado Valbuena, C. (2006) 'Hombres por la igualdad de género en un nuevo escenario social [Men for gender equality in a new social scenario]', in M.Á. Rebollo (ed) *Género e Interculturalidad: Educar para la Igualdad [Gender and Interculturality: To Teach for Gender Equality]*, Madrid: La Muralla, pp 85–122.

Delgado Valbuena, C. (2009) *Sociología del Género y de los Grupos de Edad [Sociology of Gender and Age Groups]*, Seville: Secretariado de Recursos Audiovisuales y Nuevas Tecnologías de la Universidad de Sevilla.

Egeberg Holmgren, L. (2007) 'Killing Bill: men as rebellious feminists in the politics of passing', *NORMA: Nordic Journal for Masculinity Studies*, 2(1): 16–37.

Egeberg Holmgren, L. (2011a) *IngenMansLand: Om Män som Feminister, Intervjuframträdanden och Passerandets Politik [No Man's Land: On Men as Feminists, Interview Performances and the Politics of Passing]*, Uppsala: Acta Universitatis Upsaliensis.

Egeberg Holmgren, L. (2011b) 'Co-fielding in qualitative interviews: gender, knowledge, and interaction in a study of (pro)feminist men', *Qualitative Inquiry*, 17(4): 364–78.

Egeberg Holmgren, L. (2013) 'Gendered selves, gendered subjects: interview performances and situational contexts in critical interview studies of men and masculinities', in B. Pini and B. Pease (eds) *Men, Masculinities and Methodologies*, London: Palgrave Macmillan, pp 90–102.

Egeberg Holmgren, L. and Hearn, J. (2009) 'Framing 'men in feminism': theoretical locations, local contexts and practical passings in men's gender-conscious positionings on gender equality and feminism', *Journal of Gender Studies*, 18(4): 403–18.

Ekelund, R. (forthcoming) 'Young feminist men finding their way: on young Swedish men's experiences of and orientations in feminist settings', *Culture Unbound: Journal of Current Cultural Research*, 12(3): 506–26.

Eriksson, M. (2003) *I Skuggan av Pappa: Familjerätten och Hanteringen av Fäders Våld [In the Shadow of Daddy: Family Law and the Handling of Fathers' Violence]*, Stehag: Gondolin.

Esping-Andersen, G. (1990) *The Three Worlds of Welfare Capitalism*, Cambridge: Polity Press.

Hydén, M. (2020) 'Ökning av våld i nära relation som en följd av coronapandemin [Increase in violence in close relations due to the coronapandemic]', *Forte*, Available from: www.forte.se/nyhet/okning-av-vald-nara-relationer-som-en-foljd-av-coronapandemin/ [Accessed 3 October 2020].

Fileborn, B. and Loney-Howes, R. (2019) 'Mapping the emergence of #MeToo', in B. Fileborn and R. Loney-Howes (eds) *#MeToo and the Politics of Social Change*, Cham: Palgrave Macmillan, pp 1–18.

Flood, M. (2007) 'Men's movement', in M. Flood, J.K. Gardiner, B. Pease and K. Pringle (eds) *International Encyclopedia of Men and Masculinities*, London: Routledge, pp 418–22.

Flood, M. (2011) 'Involving men in efforts to end violence against women', *Men and Masculinities*, 14(3): 358–77.

Flood, M. (2019) *Engaging Men and Boys in Violence Prevention*, Basingstoke: Palgrave Macmillan.

Flood, M., Dragiewicz, M. and Pease, B. (2020) 'Resistance and backlash to gender equality', *Australian Journal of Social Issues*, epub ahead of print 1 October 2020, DOI: 10.1002/ajs4.137.

Florin, C. and Nilsson, B. (2000) *Något Som Liknar en Oblodig Revolution: Jämställdhetens Politisering Under 1960-och 70-talen [Something Like a Bloody Revolution: Gender Politicization in the 1960s and 1970s]*, Umeå: Umeå Universitet.

Försäkringskassan [Swedish Social Insurance Agency] (2019) *Socialförsäkringen i siffor 2019 [Social insurance in figures 2019]*, Stockholm: Försäkringskassan.

Gottzén, L. (2018) 'Krisande män och kontrollerad orgasm – mansrörelsens affektiva politik [Crisis men and controlled orgasm – the affective policy of the men's movement]', *Ord Och Bild*, 127(4): 29–35.

Gottzén, L. (2019) 'Chafing masculinity: heterosexual violence and young men's shame', *Feminism & Psychology*, 29(2): 145–56.

Greig, A. (2019) *Masculinities and the Rise of the Far-Right: Implications for Oxfam's Work on Gender Justice*, Washington, DC: Oxfam America.

Guasch, O. (ed) (2012) *Vidas de Hombre(s): Relatos de Vida [Lives of Man(s): Life Stories]*, Barcelona: Bellaterra.

Harne, L. and Radford, J. (2008) *Tackling Domestic Violence: Theories, Policies and Practice*, Maidenhead: Open University Press.

Hearn, J. (1998) *The Violences of Men: How Men Talk About and How Agencies Respond to Men's Violence to Women*, London: Sage Publications.

Hearn, J. (2015) 'The uses and abuses of the political category of "men": activism, policy and theorising', in M. Flood and R. Howson (eds) *Engaging Men in Building Gender Equality*, Cambridge: Cambridge Scholars, pp 34–54.

Hearn, J. and Pringle, K. (2006) 'Men, masculinities and children: some European perspectives', *Critical Social Policy*, 26(2): 365–89.

Hearn, J., Nordberg, M., Andersson, K., Balkmar, D., Gottzén, L., Klinth, R., Pringle, K. and Sandberg, L. (2012) 'Hegemonic masculinity and beyond: 40 years of research in Sweden', *Men and Masculinities*, 15(1): 31–55.

Hart, L. and Hart, R. (2018) *Remembered Forever: Our Family's Devastating Story of Domestic Abuse and Murder*, London: Seven Dials.

Heilman, B., Barker, G. and Harrison, A. (2017) *The Man Box: A Study on Being a Young Man in the US, UK, and Mexico*, Washington, DC and London: Promundo US and Unilever.

Hester, M. (2005) 'Tackling men's violence in families: lessons for the UK', in M. Eriksson, M. Hester, S. Keskinen and K. Pringle (eds) *Tackling Men's Violence in Families: Nordic Issues and Dilemmas*, Bristol: Policy Press, pp 173–82.

Holli, A.M., Magnusson, E. and Rönnblom, M. (2005) 'Critical studies of Nordic discourses on gender and gender equality', *NORA: Nordic journal of feminist and gender research*, 13(3): 148–52.

Ishkanian, A. (2014) 'Neoliberalism and violence: The Big Society and the changing politics of domestic violence in England', *Critical Social Policy*, 43(3): 333–53.

Jewkes, R., Flood, M. and Lang, J. (2015) 'From work with men and boys to changes of social norms and reduction of inequities in gender relations: a conceptual shift in prevention of violence against women and girls', *The Lancet*, 385(9977): 1580–9.

Johansson, M., Johansson, K. and Andersson, E. (2018) '#MeToo in the Swedish forest sector: testimonies from harassed women on sexualised forms of male control', *Scandinavian Journal of Forest Research*, 33(5): 419–25.

Järvklo, N. (2008) 'En man utan penis: heteronormativitet och svensk maskulinitetspolitik [A man without penis: heteronormativity and Swedish masculinity politics]', *Lambda Nordica*, 13(4): 16–35.

Kamyab, M. and Geborek Lundberg, J. (2019) 'Men's pathway to gender equality work', Master's thesis, Stockholm: Stockholm University.

Kantola, J. (2006) *Feminists Theorize the State*, Basingstoke: Palgrave Macmillan.

Kaufman, G. and Almqvist, A.-L. (2017) 'The role of partners and workplaces in British and Swedish men's parental leave decisions', *Men and Masculinities*, 20(5): 533–51.

Kjellberg, J. (2013) 'Jämställdhet, maskulinitet och (o)privilegierade subjektspositioner: den svenska jämställdhetsdiskursens exkluderingar [Gender equality, masculinity and (un)privileged subject positions: the exclusions of Swedish gender equality discourse]', *NORMA: Nordic Journal for Masculinity Studies*, 8(2): 113–30.

Klinth, R. and Johansson, T. (2010) *Nya Svenska Fäder [New Swedish Fathers]*, Umeå: Borea Bokförlag.

Levtov, R.G., Barker, G., Contreras-Urbina, M., Heilman, B. and Verma, R. (2014) 'Pathways to gender-equitable men: findings from the international men and gender equality survey in eight countries', *Men and Masculinities*, 17(5): 467–501.

Lewis, R., Rowe, M. and Wiper, C. (2017) 'Online abuse of feminists as an emerging form of violence against women and girls', *British Journal of Criminology*, 57(6): 1462–81.

Lombardo, E. (2017) 'The Spanish gender regime in the EU context: changes and struggles in times of austerity', *Gender, Work & Organization*, 24(1): 20–33.

Lombard, N. and Whiting, N. (2015) 'Domestic abuse: feminism, the government and the unique case of Scotland', in R. Goel and L. Goodmark (eds) *Comparative Perspectives on Domestic Violence: Lessons from Efforts Worldwide*, Oxford: Oxford University Press, pp 155–68.

Lorente Acosta, M. (2008) *Mi Marido me Pega lo Normal: Agresión a la Mujer – Realidades y Mitos [My Husband Beats Me Normally: Assault on Women – Facts and Myths]* (2nd ed), Madrid: Planeta.

Lorente Acosta, M. (2009) *Los Nuevos Hombres Nuevos. Los Miedos se Siempre en Tiempos de Igualdad [The new men: The usual fears in times of equality]*, Barcelona: Destino.

Lorente Acosta, M. (2018) *Tú Haz la Comida, que yo Cuelgo los Cuadros: Trampas y Tramposos en la Cultura de la Desigualdad [You Make the Food and I Hang the Pictures: Traps and Cheats in the Culture of Inequality]*, Madrid: Crítica.

Lozoya, J.Á., Bonino, L., Leal, D. and Szil, P. (2003) 'Cronología inconclusa del movimiento de hombres igualitarios del Estado Español [Unfinished chronology of the movement of egalitarian men of the Spanish State]', Jerez: Programa Hombres por la Igualdad and Ayuntamiento de Jerez [Men for Equality Programme and Jerez City Council], Available from: http://szil.info/es/publicaciones/cronologia-inconclusa-del-movimiento-de-hombres [Accessed 28 March 2021].

Lozoya J.A., Bedoya, J.M. and Espada, C.H. (eds) (2008) 'Voces de hombres por la igualdad [Voices of men for equality]', Available from: https://vocesdehombres.wordpress.com [Accessed 29 January 2021].

Lundqvist, Å. (2013) 'Framväxten av den svenska familjepolitiken [The emergence of the Swedish family policy]', in H. Swärd, P.G. Edebalk and E. Wadensjö (eds) *Vägar till Välfärd. Idéer, Inspiratörer, Kontroverser, Perspektiv [Ways to Welfare: Ideas, Inspirations, Controversies, Perspectives]*, Stockholm: Liber.

Macomber, K. (2018) ' "I'm sure as hell not putting any man on a pedestal": male privilege and accountability in domestic and sexual violence work', *Journal of Interpersonal Violence*, 33(9): 1491–518.

Marchese, E. (2008) 'No women allowed: exclusion and accountability in men's anti-rape groups', *Journal of International Women's Studies*, 9(2): 59–76.

Martinsson, L., Griffin, G. and Nygren K.G. (eds) (2016) *Challenging the Myth of Gender Equality in Sweden*, Bristol: Policy Press.

Marqués, J.-V. (1991) *Curso Elemental para Varones Sensibles y Machistas Recuperables [Elementary Course for Sensitive Males and Recoverable Sexists]*, Madrid: Temas de Hoy.

McKinney, C. (2019) 'Sexual coercion, gender construction, and responsibility for freedom: a Beauvoirian account of #MeToo', *Journal of Women, Politics and Policy*, 40(1): 75–96.

Meadows, R. (2007) 'Epistemology', in M. Flood, J.K. Gardiner, B. Pease and K. Pringle (eds) *International Encyclopedia of Men and Masculinities*, London: Routledge, pp 173–7.

Messner, M.A., Greenberg, M.A. and Peretz, T. (2015) *Some Men: Feminist Allies in the Movement to End Violence Against Women*, Oxford: Oxford University Press.

Män för Jämställdhet/MÄN (2014) 'Etablerade verksamheter som idag arbetar med män och jämställdhet - en svensk kartläggning med internationell utblick [Established activities today working with men and gender equality – a Swedish survey with an international outlook]', Bilaga 22, in SOU 2014:6, Män och Jämställdhet [Men and Gender Equality], Stockholm: Fritzes, Available from: https://www.regeringen.se/49b70d/contentassets/6e2024c9c99948bfa0522 24089272c0e/man-och-jamstalldhet-bilaga-23-sou-20146 [Accessed 28 March 2021].

Ministerio de Igualdad (2020) 'Macroencuesta de violencia contra las mujeres 2019 [Macro survey on violence against women 2019]', Madrid: Ministry of Equality, Spanish Government.

Murphy, M.J. (2009) 'Can "men" stop rape? Visualising gender in the "my strength is not for hurting" rape prevention campaign', *Men and Masculinities*, 12(1): 113–30.

Nardini, K. (2016) 'Men's networking for gender justice: thinking through global/local strategies – starting from the Italian and Spanish cases', *Journal of Men's Studies*, 24(3): 241–58.

Nyberg, A. (2012) 'Gender equality policy in Sweden: 1970s–2010s', *Nordic Journal of Working Life Studies*, 2(4): 67–84.

Olsson, J. and Lauri, J. (2020) 'Det befriande ansvarets paradox: En studie av jämställdhetsinitiativet #killmiddag [The paradox of the liberating responsibility]', *Tidskrift för Genusvetenskap*, 41(3): 5–26.

Orantes, F. (2017) 'Una madre es para siempre [A mother is forever]', in N. Coronado (ed) *Hombres por la Igualdad [Men for Equality]*, Madrid: LoQueNoExiste, pp 31–40.

Pease, B. (2002) '(Re)constructing men's interests', *Men and Masculinities*, 5(2): 165–77.

Pease, B. (2008) 'Engaging men in men's violence prevention: Exploring the tensions, dilemmas and possibilities', Issues Paper 17, Sydney: Australian Domestic and Family Violence Clearinghouse, Available from: https://apo.org.au/sites/default/files/resource-files/2008-08/apo-nid1802.pdf [Accessed 28 March 2021].

Peretz, T. (2017) 'Engaging diverse men: an intersectional analysis of men's pathways to antiviolence activism', *Gender and Society*, 31(4): 526–48.

Pringle, K. (2005) 'Neglected issues in Swedish child protection policy and practice: age, ethnicity and gender', in M. Eriksson, M. Hester, S. Keskinen and K. Pringle (eds) *Tackling Men's Violence in Families: Nordic Issues and Dilemmas*, Bristol: Policy Press, pp 155–72.

Pringle, K. (2016) 'Doing (oppressive) gender via men's relations with children', in A. Häyrén and H. Wahlström Henriksson (eds) *Critical Perspectives on Masculinities and Relationalities: In Relation to What?*, Geneva: Springer, pp 23–34.

Pringle, K., Balkmar, D. and Iovanni, L. (2010) 'Trouble in paradise: Exploring patterns of research and policy response to men's violence in Denmark and Sweden', *NORA: Nordic Journal of Feminist and Gender Research*, 18(2): 105–21.

Pringle, K., Hearn, J., Ferguson, H., Pringle, K., Hearn, J., Ferguson, H., Kambourov, D., Kolga, V., Lattu, E., Müller, U., Nordberg, M., Novikova, I., Oleksy, E. and Rydzewska, J. (2006) *Men and Masculinities in Europe*, London: Whiting & Birch.

Reeser, T. and Gottzén, L. (2018) 'Masculinity and affect: new possibilities, new agendas', *NORMA: Nordic Journal for Masculinity Studies*, 13(3/4): 145–57.

Robb, M. and Ruxton, S. (2018) 'Young men and gender identity', in H. Montgomery and M. Robb (eds) *Children and Young People's Worlds*, Bristol: Policy Press, pp 141–56.

Rosenberg, M. (2015) *Nonviolent Communication: A Language of Life* (3rd edn), Encinitas, CA: PuddleDancer Press.

Ruxton, S., Robb, M., Featherstone, B. and Ward, M.R.M. (2019) 'Beyond male role models: Gender identities and work with young men in the UK', in M. Kulkarni and R. Jain (eds) *Global Masculinities: Interrogations and Reconstructions*, Abingdon: Routledge, pp 82–98.

Ruxton, S. and van der Gaag, N. (2013) 'Men's involvement in gender equality: European perspectives', *Gender and Development*, 21(1): 161–75.

Salazar Benítez, O. (2013) *Masculinidades y Ciudadanía: Los Hombres también Tenemos Género [Masculinities and Citizenship: Men also Have Gender]*, Madrid: Dykinson.

Salazar Benítez, O. (2018) *El Hombre que no Deberíamos ser [The Man you Should Not Become]*, Madrid, Planeta.

Seidler, V.J. (ed) (1991) *The Achilles Heel Reader*, London: Routledge.

Sowards, S.K. and Renegar, V.R. (2006) 'Reconceptualizing rhetorical activism in contemporary feminist contexts', *Howard Journal of Communications*, 17(1): 57–74.

Statens Offentliga Utredningar [State Public Reports] (2014) 'Våld i nära relationer – en folkhälsofråga [Domestic violence – A public health issue]', 49, Stockholm: Fritzes, Available from: https://www.regeringen.se/rattsliga-dokument/statens-offentliga-utredningar/2014/06/sou-201449/ [Accessed 28 March 2021].

Statens Offentliga Utredningar [State Public Reports] (2015) 'Nationell strategi mot mäns våld mot kvinnor och hedersrelaterat våld och förtryck: betänkande [National strategy against men's violence against women and honour-based violence and oppression]', 55, Stockholm: Fritzes, Available from: https://www.regeringen.se/rattsliga-dokument/statens-offentliga-utredningar/2015/06/sou-2015_55/ [Accessed 28 March 2021].

Téllez Infantes, A. (ed) (2019) *Masculinidades Igualitarias y Alternativas: Procesos, Avances y Reacciones [Egalitarian and Alternative Masculinities: Processes, Advances and Reactions]*, Valencia: Tirant lo Blanc Humaniddes.

Tolman, R.M., Casey, E.A., Allen, C.T., Carlson, J., Leek, C. and Storer, H.L. (2019) 'A global exploratory analysis of men participating in gender-based violence prevention', *Journal of Interpersonal Violence*, 34(16): 3438–65.

Trifiletti, R. (1999) 'Southern European welfare regimes and the worsening position of women', *Journal of European Social Policy*, 9(1): 49–64.

UN Women (2020) *COVID-19 and Ending Violence Against Women and Girls*. New York, NY: UN Women.

Webb, R. (2017) *How Not to Be a Boy*, Edinburgh: Canongate Books.

Westmarland, N. (2015) *Violence Against Women: Criminological Perspectives on Men's Violences*, Abingdon: Routledge.

Westwell, E. and Bunting, J. (2020) 'The regenerative culture of Extinction Rebellion: self-care, people care, planet care', *Environmental Politics*, 29(3): 546–51.

Wright, C.I. (2009) 'Men and their interventions in violence against women: Developing an institutional ethnography', Doctoral thesis, Huddersfield: University of Huddersfield.

Index

Note: Page numbers for figures appear in *italics*.